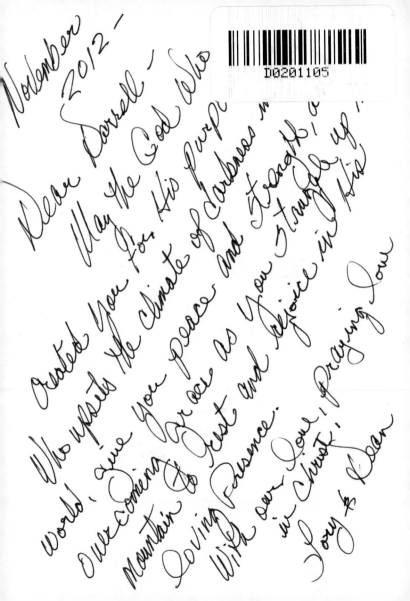

November
2012 —

Dear Darrell,

May the God Who
Created You for His Purp[ose]
Who upsets the climate of darkness in the
world. Give you peace and strength, o...
Overcoming Grace as you stand up...
Mountain to exist and rejoice in His
Loving Presence.

With our Love! Praying. Love
in Christ!

Tony & Joan

Hearing God

Lory Basham Jones

To my beloved husband, Dean
who adds the color, humor, and adventure to my life.

To our wonderful children:
Michael & Dion
Carol & Dennis
Deanna & Tom

To my precious parents, Carl & Almedia Basham

To our prized grandchildren:
Wesley and Spencer Christian
Jacob
Jared & Melissa
Michelle, David, and Bryan Anthony
and generations yet to come.

To those who listen and those who long to hear.

Published by Silver Palm Publishers, P.O. Box 570276, Tarzana, CA 91357. Printed in Colombia

The Bible version used in this publication is THE NEW KING JAMES VERSION. Copyright © 1979, 1980, 1982, Thomas Nelson, Inc., Publishers.

Library of Congress Cataloging-in-Publication Data
Jones, Lory Basham.
   Hearing God/Lory Basham Jones.
            p. cm.
   Rev. ed.
   ISBN 958-8201-00-4 • English Edition
   ISBN 958-9269-99-0 • Spanish Edition
   1. Devotional calendars. I. Title.
BV4811.J63 2002
242/.2—dc20

Introduction

What is a prophecy? That is a good question to ask, since you are holding in hand a book full of them. But it is important that you not misdefine *prophecy* as you begin to read.

First, these are not mystical, occult, faddish, or hip. They are unlike that entire genre of "prophecies" paraded before the public today.

Second, these do not pretend to be divinely inspired. Divine inspiration means prophecy is from God, given by His Holy Spirit, and intended to be received and believed as His own Word. These pages do not claim divine inspiration.

But they are divinely *prompted*. And herein lies the uniqueness, refreshing beauty, and uplifting quality of the kind of prophecy about which the New Testament Scriptures teach. For example, the first epistle to the Corinthians relates the fact that the Holy Spirit provides gifts of prophecy to profit the believer by encouragement, edification, and comfort (1 Cor. 12:7–10; 14:3). These gifts will manifest through women and men (11:5).

To people who seek Him and walk with Him daily, the Holy Spirit prompts or gives those "words," that those who hear or read them might be strengthened in Christ.

To be truly of God's Holy Spirit, they must qualify on two other points:

First, they will *align* with the whole truth of the whole Bible.

Second, they will *attract* readers to the pages of the Word of God.

No word of prophecy is valid that contradicts or twists the final revelation of the sixty-six books of the Holy Scriptures. True prophecies are consistently imbued with this trait: that their essential content is *truthfulness* and *balance* that measure up to the absolute plumb line of the Bible.

And people who understand this true spirit of prophecy will find they are drawn to the *timeless* Word of God as a result of having heard a *temporal* "word" prompted by His Spirit through the agency of one of His sons or daughters.

Lory Basham Jones is such a daughter of God. She makes no higher claim, for there is no higher human office. Her position, beside multitudes of others who have been made spiritually alive through faith in Jesus Christ, is not touted as superior to anyone else by reason of her "prophesyings." But her availability to the Holy Spirit is markedly mature. She is not a mystic or a fanatic, and is neither peculiar nor glib—just one who has a propensity for taking time to *hear* . . . and to *help*.

Dr. Jack W. Hayford
Pastor/Chancellor

The Church on the Way
The Kings College and Seminary
Van Nuys, California

iv

Foreword

"Could you not watch with Me one hour?" Jesus asked His disciples.

When my wife became sensitized by this question, she began to rise early every morning to pray. I was less impressed by the "spirituality" of her habit than with its discipline. In a Haitian missionary compound, Guatemalan jungle, tiny Thai hotel, or beneath our own comfortable covers, every morning about five, she would slide out of bed and spend an hour with the Lord.

Apparently the Lord always remembered the appointment, too, although at first, much of Lory's hour was spent being self-conscious instead of Christ-conscious. But since Jesus asked His followers to "watch"—implying a state of alertness, awareness, listening for His voice, and being on guard against any intrusion—Lory began to monitor her thoughts, discarding any that might dilute or drain her full attention from the Lord.

About a year and a half later I noticed a stack of handwritten pads on her desk. "What are these?" I asked.

"Writings from my morning prayer times," she answered.

"Do you mind if I read them?"

What I read was well grounded in Scripture, edifying, encouraging, and bringing home a fresh call to holiness.

"How many of these do you have?" I asked.

"Five or six hundred," she supposed.

"Five or six hundred?" I gasped.

"Yes, there's one for each day since I started."

Without hesitation, I blurted, "You've got a book here . . . these could be a blessing to a lot of people."

"Oh, no . . . they're so personal," she said, somewhat stunned.

I smiled. "Honey, you know God seldom does just one thing at a time. Sure, they're for us, but not exclusively. Why don't you pray about it, then submit them to mature believers and let them judge?"

So she did. And the response confirmed that what Lory was "hearing" each morning went far beyond the limitations of our own personal need for growth. She was hearing God for anyone who wanted to know Him better.

Dean Jones

January

My sheep hear My voice,
and I know them, and
they follow Me.

John 10:27

◇

Fear Not

There is no fear in love; but perfect love casts out fear, because fear involves torment. But he who fears has not been made perfect in love (1 John 4:18).

◆

Dear Lord, it is so easy to fear what lies ahead; create in me more love this year.

Fear not! for it is unbelief. And fight the good fight of faith. I have not given you a spirit of fear. As you practice My presence and let Me speak to you quietly, love will flood your being, putting fear to flight. It is not I who prepares that place; it is you. I stand at the door and knock; you have the power to open the door or keep it closed, or take it off the hinges that I may come in without knocking. (Read 2 Timothy 1:7.)

Overcoming

The thief does not come except to steal, and to kill, and to destroy. I have come that they may have life, and that they may have it more abundantly (John 10:10).

◆

Here I am again, Lord, to watch with You one hour. Happy New Year, Lord! May it, and we, be acceptable in Your sight.

Cast your cares on Me this year, and I will sustain you. It is the only way to be lighthearted and joyful when hell works to diminish all righteousness. My chosen people still wail at the western wall of the Temple grounds over the rubble of centuries past as if My immediate presence were not available to them: Jesus, the Light of the world. Just as Satan used the annihilation tactics of Hitler to try and eliminate the bloodline through which the Messiah-Redeemer came, he also used Herod to kill baby Jews in an attempt to deny you a Savior. But greater am I, saith the Lord your God, than he that is in the world. (Read 1 John 4:4.)

Criticism

Judge not, that you be not judged. For with
what judgment you judge, you will be judged;
and with the measure you use, it will be
measured back to you. And why do you look at
the speck in your brother's eye, but do not
consider the plank in your own eye? . . .
Hypocrite! First remove the plank from your
own eye, and then you will see clearly to remove
the speck from your brother's eye
(Matthew 7:1–3, 5).

◆

*Dear Jesus, I am so tired. Help me to be impartial
and uncritical today. Let Your virtue loose upon me.*

You shall be filled, My child. You shall
laugh. Blessed are you today. Leap for joy! Love
everyone, even those who criticize you . . . who
give nothing in return. Be merciful, as I am merciful. Forgive instantly. Please, please, please,
judge not, and you will not be judged. Perfect
yourself before you look critically at others.
Then you will be clear to see with spiritual eyes
how to help another. (Read Psalm 51:10.)

Courage

He who dwells in the secret place of the Most High shall abide under the shadow of the Almighty. I will say of the LORD, "He is my refuge and my fortress; My God, in Him I will trust." Surely He shall deliver you from the snare of the fowler and from the perilous pestilence (Psalm 91:1–3).

◆

O Spirit of Truth, give me Your ever-needed word of assurance that all is well.

Relax! All is well. Why should you be concerned for the icy cold of the Jordan when I aim to turn it into living water around you? Without taking away your awareness, I will give you surging and overwhelming joy. I will comfort you and sustain you in the midst of threats or temptations. Doubt not. Worry not. Fret not. Simply trust and obey. Walk in peace . . . make courage your choice. (Read Psalm 34:4.)

◇

Rest in Me

**Thus says the LORD to you: "Do not be afraid
nor dismayed because of this great multitude,
for the battle is not yours, but God's"
(2 Chronicles 20:15b).**

♦

*O Lord, thank You for awakening me. I confess
I am so tired. Give me the strength this day to overcome evil and do good . . . to overcome hurt.*

My child, I feel your weariness. Let My
peace flow over you like a river. When Jesus'
body grew weary—just like yours—He withdrew
from the crowds to commune with Me. So, too,
must you. Let neither care nor worry block the
channel . . . nor lack of love, even when you are
hurt by one you love most. If you leave it to Me,
you will not have to fight the battle. I will deal
with that one's heart, that one's temptations,
and your own suspicions. Yours is but to rest in
Me—loving, giving, not judging. Rest your
nerves. Tired nerves reflect on Me. Let your
peace reflect My power instead. (Read Psalm
34:14.)

Humility

**By humility and the fear of the LORD are riches
and honor and life (Proverbs 22:4).**

✦

Lord, help me to be unaffected by fearsome circumstances.

Your lack of fully trusting Me causes you to
be afraid; then you try and work things out by
yourself. But humility and reverence toward Me
will render riches and honor and life. You are
learning more and more to rely on Me. More
and more you know that I am the source of all
you desire. (Read Hebrews 4:7.)

January 7

◇

Vulnerable Heart

Be diligent to present yourself approved to
God, a worker who does not need to be
ashamed, rightly dividing the word
of truth (2 Timothy 2:15).

◆

*Lord Jesus, I feel so good, so warm, so lovely in
my new clothes. Help me to feel Your warmth, Your
goodness, Your loveliness even closer than my clothing . . . the freshness of our relationship more than
the excitement of a new purchase. Indeed, my Lord,
You have purchased it all—all that is necessary, and
gifts besides, and eternity as well.*

I love to give good gifts to My children.
These times of prayer and Bible-reading work in
you the patience and holiness you so desire, and
are needful for My power to be used creatively
for good. A vulnerable heart is all I need to make
you more like Me. And the more like Me, the
more you love; and as your love grows, so does
your ability to reach out to others. Be sharply
aware and ready, an instrument in My hand.
(Read James 1:17.)

As a Little Child

**Assuredly, I say to you, whoever does not
receive the kingdom of God as a little child
will by no means enter it (Mark 10:15).**

◆

*Lord, give us the power to see with spiritual eyes,
to deliver those who are in bondage to the enemy, to
free from the past those who already know You, to heal
the sick.*

The devils are subject to My children now,
through the name of Jesus; you have power over
all satanic powers, for "He who is in you is
greater than he who is in the world." It is not
to great intellects that I reveal these things but
to childlike, receptive hearts. Be less self-
conscious and more aware of Me. Do not protect yourself against Me; but as a little child,
raise your eyes to Me, knowing that I will never
take My hand away. I will lead you all the time.
Only you can break that bond. I never will! I
will stay with you always. (Read Matthew 10:8.)

January 9

◇

Forgiveness

**Judge not, and you shall not be judged.
Condemn not, and you shall not be
condemned. Forgive, and you will
be forgiven (Luke 6:37).**

◆

*Precious Father, Lord Jesus, Holy Spirit of God,
forgive us all our sins. . . .*

After you have been forgiven *all* your sins,
the best way to keep our relationship fresh is to
confess and repent quickly, as soon as you become aware of the iniquity. Be cleansed moment to moment. You are learning to do this,
and that is how you can be an inspiration to
others when it seems you have not spoken in
any meaningful way. I say to you . . . it is by My
Spirit! A cleansed spirit, uncluttered by uncon-
fessed sin, is inspiring. It is not so much what
you say but your submitted spirit, mind, and
emotions that I use to stir others to obedience.
Be constant in your repentance and eager in
your forgiveness, of yourself as well as others.
(Read Psalm 24:3–4 and 2 Corinthians 3:17.)

Light

**The fear of man brings a snare, but whoever
trusts in the LORD shall be safe
(Proverbs 29:25).**

◆

*Lord, I am sorry I do not extend myself more to
others.*

Regret not. You do not see the bright shining of your light. I do. When your eye is single toward Me, your whole body is full of light. Words are not the only way My light is transmitted. But My followers must always take care not to use My light for their own purposes. Be in no way a hypocrite like the "religious" who make clean the outside, yet leave their inward parts full of impurity and wickedness. Always speak the truth. And be not afraid of what people think; that will cause you to dilute the truth. (Read Luke 11:33–36.)

January 11

◇

Responsibility

Therefore let us not sleep, as others do, but let us watch and be sober (1 Thessalonians 5:6).

◆

Lord, I want to be rich toward You, not considering unduly what I shall eat or wear, or how I shall appear. You provide for the birds who have no storehouse, and dress the lilies in peaceful beauty. Cause all my wakeful hours and subconscious sleeping to be spent in seeking You and Your kingdom, confident that it is Your good pleasure to protect us and to press into our hands all we need, with gifts added to it.

Blessed are My servants who are watchful, for their homes shall not be broken by the enemy. Do not indulge yourself even for a moment in disobedience or rebelliousness, for truly these are spirits of darkness who come to steal your peace and joy, and ultimately bind and destroy you. Prepare yourself. Unto whom much is given, much shall be required. Discern the times, use your authority, and let Me do great and mighty things through you. (Read Luke 12:48.)

Humility

**For whoever exalts himself will be humbled,
and he who humbles himself will be
exalted (Luke 14:11).**

◆

*Thank You for healing my throat in the midst of
the meeting last night, even though I was so weary I
could hardly keep my eyes open. O Lord, help me never
to limit You and Your power, even when it comes to
carrying my cross.*

It is to the humble that I come, My child.
Whosoever exalts himself shall be abased and he
that humbles himself shall be exalted and
blessed and recompensed. You are seeking My
help for your cross and I am making your burden light. Through hard circumstances you will
learn to be at peace, calm in every situation.
Hear Me, dear one, with your eyes and ears,
with your soul and spirit: get out of My way,
and I will do great and mighty things through
you. I have said it, and I will perform it. (Read
Matthew 11:30.)

January 13

◇

Know My Joy

I say to you that likewise there will be more joy
in heaven over one sinner who repents than
over ninety-nine just persons who need
no repentance (Luke 15:7).

◆

*Thank You, Lord, for restoring us to health, and
for returning the lost.*

I rejoice when you are joyful, for that joy is
by My Spirit to you . . . and I would that you
rejoice with Me when the dead and lost of the
world are found and made alive. Know the joy
that abounds in heaven and in the presence of
the angels over one sinner who repents. Look
with great compassion on those who waste their
very lives, their spirits starving and afraid, not
even knowing what they hunger and thirst for.
Pray for their hearts to be softened, for you
know not how many prayers have gone to the
throne of God for your own soul . . . and be
faithful to all I show you. To the degree you are
faithful in the least things will you be faithful in
much. (Read Luke 15:6 and Matthew 25:23.)

Seek My Help

You ask and do not receive, because you ask amiss, that you may spend it on your pleasures (James 4:3).

◆

Lord, give comfort to those left bereft by tragedy; and in the midnight of our sorrows, Lord, be our friend. Let us not blame You for disaster but lay the blame on Satan, where it belongs, or at the door of sin and human error. You designed us perfectly, Lord; help us to follow Your plan.

I am man's present help in days of trouble. I have My hand extended as far as I can without infringing upon that precious part of man which makes him more than the animals and computerized machines—free will and choice. But man must ask, in order to be given; and seek, that he may find. Whoever knocks shall find an opening to the wholeness of My Spirit, the secrets of My Kingdom, and all authority needed to thwart the adversary. I go before and behind. (Read Luke 11:9–10.)

January 15

◇

Watch!

Watch therefore, and pray always that you may be counted worthy to escape all these things that will come to pass, and to stand before the Son of Man (Luke 21:36).

◆

Lord, let me not miss Your visitation. I want to be available all the time, so that I don't have to know the time You're coming. Put a guard on my tongue, O Lord, and allow me not to transgress with my mouth. Teach me to perceive craftiness in others, that I be not deceived; yet let me be harmless in my suspicions. And let me not be snared by flattery, for it is cunning.

Then be watchful, beloved, always on guard, strengthened by the words I speak to you. Let nothing that you have already learned dry up and die. Let all of My instruction be freshly kindled and sparked anew. Allow your mind to entertain nothing less than what is true, striking a blow against anything phony or dishonest. Keep My word and I will keep you from the hour of temptation. (Read 1 Peter 4:7.)

January 16

◇

Faith

"Blessed is she who believed, for there will be a
fulfillment of those things which were told her
from the Lord." And Mary said: "My soul
magnifies the Lord, and my spirit has rejoiced
in God my Savior" (Luke 1:45–47).

◆

*Lord, Zechariah doubted Your word that Elizabeth
would have a son. Did You silence his lips that he not
speak doubt until You had accomplished it? Would
his doubts have influenced Elizabeth? The birth of
John the Baptist? Or Mary, the mother of Jesus?*

Let Mary be your example in believing, for
without faith it is impossible to please Me.
Blessed is the one who believes and speaks what
I speak. Focus your attention on My Word.
Then you can cooperate more fully in bringing
it to pass. Trust Me. I will share My glorious rev-
elations with you as you can bear them. Conquer all doubt! My love and power will deliver
you from fear and give you poise, soul balance,
and courage. Bathe your spirit in faith. (Read
Romans 4:20–21.)

◇

Responsibility

**By your patience possess your souls
(Luke 21:19).**

◆

Lord, I am so slow to learn full control over my mind and emotions, over my thought life. Yet, I thank You for what You have already worked in my soul.

Look up, lift your head, for your full redemption of soul draws near. As you abide in Me, practice My presence, and live out My Word, you fashion a thicker shield of faith. So be quick to learn! For every worry or impatience, care or fear that enters your mind, apply My cleansers of praise, love, and trust *immediately*. Bring into captivity every thought, for your adversary chooses to rule first in the mind and emotions. Let the mind of Christ rule in you. Cast down every thought which creates fear and doubt. Do not strive. Do not rush. In your patience, you will possess your soul; and your heart will never fail for fear. (Read 2 Corinthians 10:4–5.)

Overcoming

**Hereafter the Son of Man will sit on the right
hand of the power of God (Luke 22:69).**

◆

*Dear Jesus, keep me from being other than trans-
parent, and less than loving. Help me to overcome selfish pride. Give me greater power for self-control,
patience, and honesty.*

Beloved, you make a great assault on Satan
when you arise to pray. I told My disciples to
pray, lest they enter into temptation. Allow Me
into each situation where you are less than I
have purposed, and I will make you more. My
Son sits at My right hand interceding for you,
loving you, knowing your need even before you
ask. And My Holy Spirit within you gives you
liberty and freedom in all things. Be released in
your spirit. (Read 1 John 5:7 and 1 Corinthians
3:17.)

January 19

◇

Grace

And of His fullness we have all received, and grace for grace. For the law was given through Moses, but grace and truth came through Jesus Christ (John 1:16–17).

◆

Open my understanding, Lord, that I may communicate creatively . . . and give me grace to act and react in a godly manner.

I have given you grace to sustain you . . . that great gift which you cannot earn or receive by striving, for it is a gift. The law was given by Moses, but grace and truth come by My Son, Jesus Christ, who came to declare Me and defeat evil. Let My Son's life and light shine into every dark corner. This is the day that I have made. Rejoice, and be glad in it. (Read 2 Corinthians 12:9.)

Seeking

Then Jesus turned, and seeing them following, said to them, "What do you seek?" They said to Him, "Rabbi" (which is to say, when translated, Teacher), "where are You staying?" He said to them, "Come and see." They came and saw where He was staying, and remained with Him that day (now it was about the tenth hour) (John 1:38–39).

◆

"What do you seek?" are Your first recorded words in this Gospel, Lord. Your far-seeing eyes burn into mine today, asking that same question. And I say: I am seeking You, Lord Jesus, and freedom from myself.

You have come, and you have seen. Now I say: Follow Me. Why are you troubled? Why do anxious thoughts arise in your heart? Peace be unto you. Do not allow your mind and emotions to block the beauty that is already manifest in your spirit. Rest today. Dwell in Me. And you will be free of yourself. (Read Philippians 4:6.)

January 21

◇

Obedience

His mother said to the servants, "Whatever He says to you, do it" (John 2:5).

♦

Dear Jesus, Your mother's last recorded words were: "Whatever He says to you, do it." Lord, I want always to be found doing what You say. You want to perform miracles. I want to listen and obey.

Yes. My hour is come. This is the time. Even today you will experience release. At peace, you will not think more highly of man's appraisals than you ought, or care too much how you appear to this one or that. Say often: "He must increase and I must decrease." When any debilitating thoughts try to enter, cast them instantly away. I will keep you in perfect peace when your mind stays on Me. Practice pulling your thoughts back more and more to that quiet place of security and serenity, where My Holy Spirit can flow through you. (Read Isaiah 26:3.)

Responsibility

**And this is the condemnation, that the light
has come into the world, and men loved
darkness rather than light, because their
deeds were evil (John 3:19).**

♦

*Precious Lord, thank You for teaching me to lis-
ten. Continue to help me know Your Word and hear
Your Holy Spirit, giving up my own preconceived no-
tions as You give me new light and truth.*

Faith is required for surrender. Know Me as
the Savior, not the condemner, of the world.
The condemnation is that light is come into the
world, and men love darkness instead . . . most
for fear that their deeds will come to light. That
fear comes from the accuser, the father of lies,
the condemner, Satan. Let your love and light
shine into those dark corners, routing fear and
other supernatural spirits of the arena of hell
that rob poor souls of the truth. Speak My
words, minister faith, deliver, heal, prophesy,
and show others what I am like. (Read Luke
10:19.)

January 23

◇

Healing Virtue

For she said, "If only I may touch His clothes,
I shall be made well." Immediately the fountain
of her blood was dried up, and she felt in
her body that she was healed of the
affliction (Mark 5:28–29).

◆

Dear Lord, I draw close to You . . . cover me.

Never fear that I will not be here. As you
draw close to Me, My virtue spills over you as
water over a river rock—cleansing, refreshing,
healing, and lubricating. It was so for the
woman who touched the hem of My garment.
I did not command the virtue to flow. It was an
automatic thing, as she drew near to Me, believing. Come and drink of Me and you shall
never thirst. Worship Me in spirit and in truth.
You must prepare your mind and emotions, but
pure worship comes only through the spirit, for
I am Spirit. Set your spirit free, that it might
worship Me. (Read John 4:23–24.)

Rejoice Always!

**Rejoice always, pray without ceasing, in
everything give thanks; for this is the
will of God in Christ Jesus for you
(1 Thessalonians 5:16–18).**

◆

*Lord Jesus, You asked the man at Bethesda pool,
"Do you want to be made well?" When he received,
You said, "See, you have been made well. Sin no
more, lest a worse thing come upon you." Tell us, I
pray, how to stay well and whole.*

The proverb is true that says, "A merry heart
does good, like medicine, a broken spirit dries
the bones." To stay whole, rejoice always! (Read
Proverbs 15:13 and 17:22.)

Humility

You are worthy, O Lord, to receive glory and honor and power; for You created all things, and by Your will they exist and were created (Revelation 4:11).

◆

My Lord, the Way, the Truth and the Life, great Master of order, organization, and discipline—show me how to commune with You joyfully all the time.

Know ahead what your plan is, as I knew ahead that we would feed the five thousand or that I would speak to the woman at the well. Be ready! Always allow Me to control your thoughts—never tense or impatient or anxious— and such power and understanding, insight and vision, peace and compassion shall be yours, beyond your greatest desires. And when these things come to pass, do not stay to receive the glory, but pass it on to Him who exalted you. Depart into that place where you are alone with the Father, where you praise and honor Him, and give Him the credit. Therein is joy everlasting. (Read 2 Corinthians 9:8.)

Calm and Confident

Rather let it be the hidden person of the heart,
with the incorruptible beauty of a gentle and
quiet spirit, which is very precious in the
sight of God (1 Peter 3:4).

♦

*O Lord, teach me to pray as I ought . . . to praise,
to wait, to confess and repent, to pray by the Scriptures . . . according to Your will always. Liberate me
from me; let me not be open to self-deception, but only
to Your presence. Make my noisy places silent.*

Dear one, silence comes from practice. It is
a way of the heart, from a spirit that is calm and
uncluttered. Your great task is to disallow ruffled
feelings even a moment's residence. Stop all activity to free yourself from a fretful moment . . .
until absolute calm returns. But first you must
be able to wait . . . for the fruit meant for ripen-
ing in July will not be ready in April. (Read Isaiah 30:15.)

◇

Only My Will

Having made known to us the mystery of His
will, according to His good pleasure which He
purposed in Himself, that in the dispensation
of the fullness of the times He might gather
together in one all things in Christ, both
which are in heaven and which are on
earth (Ephesians 1:9–10).

◆

*Holy Spirit of God, give me righteous dreams to
dream. Embolden me to expect the fulfillment of Your
deep and lofty ideas in my life.*

Not only do I give you dreams, but I bring
them to fruition. If you would know what is
yours and what is Mine, bring all and lay it on
the altar. What is Mine, I bring about. Have I
not said, "Call to Me, and I will answer you,
and show you great and mighty things, which
you do not know"? (Read Jeremiah 33:3.)

◇

Be Not Deceived

**Then Jesus spoke to them again, saying, "I am
the light of the world. He who follows Me
shall not walk in darkness, but have
the light of life" (John 8:12).**

◆

*Dear Jesus, You permeate and brighten every-
thing in my world. Give me Your instruction today.*

I am truly the light of life. And those who
know Me shall not walk in darkness. Follow
Me. Do as I do. Do not let Satan lie to you, nor
convey any of his lusts to you. Open your ears.
Everyone who hears My words and honors
them shall never see death. The body may die,
but that is not the life I speak of. It is your spirit,
breathed into by My Holy Spirit, which is eternal. So be at peace. Seek to know My character
and emulate it more and more. If you have seen
Me you have seen the Father, for We are One.
Honor the Father with *all* glory. If you take the
glory yourself, your honor is nothing but dead-
ness. (Read John 8:47 and 11:26.)

Obedience

**As long as I am in the world, I am the
light of the world (John 9:5).**

◆

*Lord, help us to work the works of our Father as
Jesus did.*

As long as Jesus was in the world, He was
the light of the world . . . and still is; yet He
sits at My right hand constantly interceding for
those I can use to be lights in the world. To
those who will, I say: Be cleansed, go, receive
more; obedience is the precursor of miracles. I
say: Prophesy in My name. I say: Greater works
than His shall you do, because He is with Me.
And always I say: Do as He did when on earth—
give Me the praise, the honor, and the glory.
Here is a marvelous thing, for it is I who exalt
you. Love My Son, the Bright and Morning
Star, who has awakened you to Me, the Father.
I sent Him that those who see not might see.
You are the extension of Him. You go. Be an
awakener. I am present. My Spirit is in you.
What more do you need? (Luke 10:21–24.)

Resurrection Life

I am the door. If anyone enters by Me, he
will be saved, and will go in and out and
find pasture (John 10:9).

♦

*Dear Lord, in my dream I struggled up a steep
cliff to get to the dining area, when I could have
walked in by the door. Yet You welcomed me with a
smile, and recognized me as one of Your sheep, and
asked, "Why did you come up the hard way?" Go
before me now, Lord; lead out the easy way and I will
follow, for I know Your voice.*

Yes, I am the door of the sheep. Satan comes
to steal, kill, and destroy but I am come to give
you life—more abundant, more freeing, more
liberating. I enter as the truth, and I will never
leave you nor forsake you. I laid down My life
as proof that what I say is true. And I was given
power to take it up again . . . and give it to you.
Receive My resurrection life! That same power
is yours. Believe, believe! You are My lamb. Listen to My voice! (Read John 10:1–2.)

January 31

◇

By My Spirit

Jesus said to her, "I am the resurrection and the life. He who believes in Me, though he may die, he shall live" (John 11:25).

♦

Lord, after all Your inspiration yesterday, this morning I feel spent and irritable . . . and everyone else seems to have problems, too. Help us!

I am the Resurrection and the Life. I raise up that which is dead and give life where there is none. These things you hold before Me shall be accomplished not by might, nor by power, but by My Spirit. But you must allow Me . . . daily. Love, joy, and peace are Spirit attributes, miracle-producing, found in that quiet place of retreat with Me; and they bring forth all that is needed to be fruitful, creative, and successful on the physical, spiritual, and mental planes. I am the wall of fire. I encompass you—and those you love and pray for—as the protector. My glory surrounds you as the air you breathe. Sing and rejoice, dear one, for I have places for you to walk among the angels. (Read Zechariah 3:7.)

February

Then you will call upon Me
and go and pray to Me,
and I will listen to you.

Jeremiah 29:12

February 1

◇

Go Forward Unafraid

And let the peace of God rule in your hearts, to which also you were called in one body; and be thankful (Colossians 3:15).

◆

Father, why is it so hard to make decisions? Thank You that You are my decision maker.

I have prepared you, and I will guide you. Go forward unafraid! And let My peace act as the umpire to all your decisions. Start fresh today! Be free of burdens or worries, for you have not gained godly wisdom or knowledge to carry the load of the Holy One. Do not fret. Leave all to Me. Just open your hands to receive the lovely treasure I have for you. But remember that the precious is to be handled gently, not clutched or crushed with worry and fear. Be glad. Let your heart quiver with excitement. I can only bless the willing. (Read Proverbs 30:3.)

Godly Character

**Most assuredly, I say to you, unless a grain
of wheat falls into the ground and dies, it
remains alone; but if it dies, it produces
much grain (John 12:24).**

◆

*In the shaky foundation of life and governments,
You are our sure foundation, King Jesus, our strength
and protection. Help us to be free of those divisive traits
which cause dissension, and to take on more of Your
holy character traits.*

Unless you die to self, you abide alone; but
if you die, you bring forth much fruit. Follow
Me. Where I am there is life and power. When
you serve Me, My Father honors you, for He
sent Me to show you what He is like. If you
would develop in godly character, do not worry
about what people say of you. Do not think
more highly of them or yourself than you
ought. Simply believe in Me . . . walk quietly
before Me. And I will instruct you in discretion.
I am wonderful in counsel, and excellent in
working. (Read Hebrews 11:6.)

Relinquishment

A new commandment I give to you, that you love one another; as I have loved you, that you also love one another. By this all will know that you are My disciples, if you have love for one another (John 13:34–35).

◆

O Lord, my refiner and purifier, help me to keep a cheerful countenance while You are at work in me.

Will you serve Me gladly? There are so many who serve Me with long faces and furrowed brows, and I will receive them gladly. But I say again that My yoke is easy and My burden is light. That which makes the load easy and light is joy and love. My power is My love. Receive power. I took the uniform of a slave and laid down My security, identity, and authority to wash My disciples' feet. Let your goal be as Mine—total redemption. I have paid the all-inclusive price. Lay down your own life. Love is the power by which it is done. (Read 1 Corinthians 13:13.)

Love

He who has My commandments and keeps them, it is he who loves Me. And he who loves Me will be loved by My Father, and I will love him and manifest Myself to him (John 14:21).

♦

Lord, how can I know when I am truly loving You and not just following a pattern I've learned? I want to believe fully, trust You wholly, and love You with all my heart.

Let not your heart be troubled. You are not an orphan who is comfortless and afraid, for I have adopted you and made you My own. Stop acting as if I will reject you. My Father loves you, and I love you. Love is the pattern for living, a habit . . . just stay open to Me all the time. The greatest commandment is that you love Me with all that is in you (proof of that love is that you keep My commandments), and love your neighbor as yourself. My Holy Spirit will teach you all you need to know about love, will keep your memory bright, and will give you peace. (Read John 14:22–23.)

February 5

◇

Cleansed by My Word

**Abide in Me, and I in you. As the branch
cannot bear fruit of itself, unless it abides
in the vine, neither can you, unless you
abide in Me (John 15:4).**

◆

*O Lord, cleanse my heart of any guile or iniquity,
and make me altogether good in Your sight.*

Be open to receive with meekness My *Logos*—
the entirety of My Word—for you are made clean
through the washing of the Word. You can neither hear nor abide, unless you stay constantly
open to Me. I am the vine, your source of all life,
all creativity, all growth. My purging is not pu-
nitive nor wrathful, but it is a universal retribu-
tion for turning from My love—a law set in
motion, like gravity. I warn My children of the
dangers as you warn your children of the hurt
of fire. Without Me, you wither. With Me, you
grow and produce much fruit. Herein is My Father glorified. And when you ask for My
rhema—a specific Word—you shall have it. Continue in My love. (Read John 15:1–9.)

Love

These things I have spoken to you, that My joy may remain in you, and that your joy may be full (John 15:11).

◆

O Lord, my strength, lift Yourself, a scepter, and let Your authority be seen in our home. Make our dwelling place strong, like a nest built in a rock: a place to hear Your words, receive Your knowledge, see visions, and dream dreams.

If you keep My commandments, your joy will be full and complete, and that joy will make you strong. Those who live in My love also love one another. You are My friends. Friends, I say, for I confide in you everything My Father has told Me. Love one another so the world will know. And pray for those who have not yet filled up their heart's vacuum with Me, for I love each one just as I love you. (Read Nehemiah 8:10.)

◇

Peace

They will put you out of the synagogues; yes, the time is coming that whoever kills you will think that he offers God service (John 16:2).

♦

Lord, all time belongs to You, yet I often feel hurried and rushed. Show me how to order my time to accomplish peacefully all that needs to be done.

Beloved, the time is coming when whoever kills you will think that he does Me a service. In Me, you have peace. If you cannot receive My peace to go from one thing to the next now, when your freedom is not endangered, where will your peace be in those days? How can you be content and of good cheer in such times if you have not learned to be at ease, graceful and poised, welcoming interruption, in such blessed times as these? Think on this often. This is life eternal that you are living in now. Enjoy it! (Read Psalm 101:2.)

◇

Patience

Pilate therefore said to Him, "Are You a king then?" Jesus answered, "You say rightly that I am a king. For this cause I was born, and for this cause I have come into the world, that I should bear witness to the truth. Everyone who is of the truth hears My voice" (John 18:37).

◆

Dear Lord Jesus, to this end were You born, that You should bear witness to the truth. And everyone who is of the truth hears Your voice. Help me to listen patiently for Your voice and bear witness to Your truth.

The moment you realize I am your supply, you will know My power. As you seek Me, you will hear My voice. Be patient; My truthfulness will flow from you. Allow no anxiety or fear to destroy your trust in Me or your ability to hear Me. Be constant in hope. Be filled up with Me in a spirit of praise, and be assured My timing is perfect. (Read Psalm 27:14.)

February 9

◇

Wasteful Thinking

Fight the good fight of faith, lay hold on eternal life, to which you were also called and have confessed the good confession in the presence of many witnesses (1 Timothy 6:12).

◆

Lord Jesus, give me light on absentminded, daydreamy thoughts that keep separating me from You.

Man does not want to face the reality of spiritual darkness, for it makes him see his own sin. So, instead of confronting the reality of My holiness, he allows absentmindedness, daydreaming, wandering, and unproductive thinking to cause a retreat into a make-believe world. Fight! As often as you must, fight to maintain the association with Me that will cause your days and hours not to be in vain. Ask the Holy Spirit to admonish you when you begin to lose yourself in wasteful thinking, and to give you a dread of everything that seeks to interrupt our union. (Read Proverbs 4:23.)

Vigilance

**Therefore my heart is glad, and my glory
rejoices; my flesh also will rest in
hope (Psalm 16:9).**

◆

*David said, "My sin is always before me"; and
also, "I have set the LORD always before me." Lord,
I know that Satan accuses and reminds us of past failures, but I ask that when I have repented and been
forgiven, all I will see before me is You.*

Let your soul rejoice, your tongue give
thanks, your flesh rest in hope, for I have sent
the Holy Spirit to keep you from following the
way of the world or being ruled by past failures.
And I have sent My Word, that you may continue steadfastly. Give up your own way, proclaim My power over your inability, and keep
your heart with all vigilance, for from it flow the
springs of life. If you still lack the humility to be
comfortable in any circumstance, seek to be
more truthful, with an honesty that can stand
the challenge of the world . . . and My heavenly
searchlight, too! (Read Luke 11:13.)

February 11

◇

Waiting

Therefore the LORD will wait, that He may be gracious to you; and therefore He will be exalted, that He may have mercy on you. For the LORD is a God of justice; blessed are all those who wait for Him (Isaiah 30:18).

◆

Lord, show me how to wait upon You and Your timing, without anxiety and ceaseless motion.

Fasten your eyes on Me. Not with a shortened, nearsighted gaze, or with a faraway look in your eye, but with a true perspective. See and know the reality that nothing is created or held together except by Me. That is the great reality. To what lesser power would you say Yes, and give love and honor involving your whole heart, your whole mind, soul, and strength? Beloved, what a privilege to be asked to wait for one hour, wait on Me who made you for My pleasure. Leap to praise Me . . . I know you best and love you most. I have chosen you for My own. (Read Isaiah 40:31.)

Boldness

**And when they had prayed, the place where
they were assembled together was shaken;
and they were all filled with the Holy Spirit,
and they spoke the word of God with
boldness (Acts 4:31).**

◆

*Lord, show me how to fill up and link up with
You—in prayer, in power, in purpose, in partnership.*

I will give you boldness to speak just as I did
Peter and John; as they were filled with the
Holy Ghost, so are you filled. And when unbelievers and criticizers see your boldness to speak,
they will know that you, too, have been with
Me. Great grace and explosive power I give to
you, and you shall lack nothing that you need
to perform every work and finish every task to
which I have called you. Have no fear! Life is
really consciousness of Me. Live now! It is life
eternal! (Read Joshua 1:9.)

February 13

◇

Praise and Work

**Now hope does not disappoint, because the love
of God has been poured out in our hearts
by the Holy Spirit who was given
to us (Romans 5:5).**

◆

*This morning I sing of Your great blessings. Oh,
great heart . . . how much You love us. Help us to
love You back, our propitiation, our Lord.*

Your song of praise is a sweet sound in My
ear. Remember to honor My Spirit as well, by
whom My love illumines your marriage, your
relationships. As you work together for good,
many will be added to Me and many will be
healed. But you must be tuned in to the fre-
quency of My Spirit. As you speak the words of
your testimony and experience, and what I have
spoken to you by My Spirit and the Scriptures,
you shall see those who are imprisoned and
chained to Satan freed. My work will never be
overthrown, for I am God. Let it be said of your
works: They cannot be overthrown, for they are
of God. (Read Acts 5:1–11 and 1 John 2:2.)

Vulnerable Heart

**But seek first the kingdom of God and His
righteousness, and all these things shall
be added to you (Matthew 6:33).**

◆

*Our faithful and true witness, make me a person
of faith and obedience, one who operates with integrity
and humility, single purpose and selflessness.*

Heaven is My throne, and earth is My foot-
stool. My hands have made all that is. What you
have asked is the simplest, easiest thing for Me
to perform, because your heart is open and willing for My manifest power and glory to fill you
all in all. Remain vulnerable. Keep your mind
and heart free of clutter, free of any selfish mo-
tive. Keep coming to Me to be energized, transformed. Your greatest work is done alone with
Me; outward tasks flow freely from our union
of spirit. (Read Ephesians 3:14–19.)

February 15

◇

Surprise Attack

Be sober, be vigilant; because your adversary
the devil walks about like a roaring lion,
seeking whom he may devour (1 Peter 5:8).

◆

*O Lord, open our eyes to see more clearly into the
realm of darkness. Help us to be sober and vigilant
and ever watchful.*

Yes, be sober and vigilant, aware of your adversary's many forms, camouflages, and approaches, alert to his timing. He will always attempt the surprise attack to get you on the run. Recognize him, confront him, and stand your ground; you will be the conqueror! When you resist him, he must flee from you. That's the way it is, for thus "it is written." (Read James 4:7.)

Let Me Increase

Then your light shall break forth like the morning, your healing shall spring forth speedily, and your righteousness shall go before you; the glory of the LORD shall be your rear guard (Isaiah 58:8).

◆

The atmosphere is filled with chaos this morning. Let us look up and see Your glory, Lord.

Believe with all your heart. My glory surrounds you, is always with you, and goes in and out with you as you glorify Me. The world does not need supermen and wonderwomen but supernatural men and women who will persistently let My divine power work through them. Allow My creativity and inspiration to take the place of worldly ambition. Know that the work is Mine alone and you shall be used mightily. Stand still, and know that I am God. I change not. I am the same every day. (Read Psalm 46:10.)

February 17

◇

Quality Time

**You are worthy, O Lord, to receive glory and
honor and power; for You created all things,
and by Your will they exist and were
created (Revelation 4:11).**

◆

Here I am Lord, to "watch" with You again.

O My dearest, you have no idea what this
time alone with Me means. It is a feeding time
for your mind and emotions, by the One who
created you. How I yearn for those with whom
I can communicate. So often, those who do
speak to Me have one foot out the door as they
come to Me for help. How rude and hurtful it
would be for a friend to be treated so. What
kind of friend would always come—only for a
moment—to ask for something, then be off to
another destination? This time is precious to
you, yes, even a necessity; for Me, it is a pleasure. I love you. I receive your praise. (Read
Psalm 16:11.)

Judgment

Far be it from You to do such a thing as this, to slay the righteous with the wicked, so that the righteous should be as the wicked; far be it from You! Shall not the Judge of all the earth do right? (Genesis 18:25).

◆

O Lord, I have so often wondered what happens to those "kind and just" people who have gone before, who did not know You.

Will the Judge of the universe not do right, my child? I will deal fairly with these in the day when I judge the secrets of men and women by Jesus Christ according to My gospel. I am not a respecter of persons. In every nation, there are those who fear Me, and work righteousness and are acceptable to Me. And Him whom I raised on the third day, anointed of the Holy Ghost and with power, shall judge the quick and the dead. And whoever believes in Him shall receive remission of sins. (Read Romans 2:1–16.)

◇

Faith

**The steps of a good man are ordered by the
LORD, and He delights in his way
(Psalm 37:23).**

◆

*Lord, I thank You for Your sustaining grace, for
upholding me when situations are beyond me, and for
giving confidence to go forward when I am afraid.*

Every one of your cries is heard. You may be
unable to see it immediately, but you shall see
and be thankful that One who sees and knows
all, the end from the beginning, is taking care of
you. So, go forward unafraid, for it is as certain
that I will see your affairs are ordered, as to see
that the sun will set in the West this evening.
Each time I place you in an uncomfortable atmosphere or circumstance, it is to train you, to
discipline you, to strengthen your faith. I will
not, I cannot fail you. Live in every detail of the
things I have said to you. And you shall be successful in your spirit, mind, and body. Be restored and rested and ever conscious of Me.
(Read Psalm 37:24–25.)

Only Believe

**For if you forgive men their trespasses, your
heavenly Father will also forgive you
(Matthew 6:14).**

◆

*Lord, I want to be devout and honorable, to glorify You and Your holy Word. Thy face, Lord, will I
seek.*

You are one after My own heart, and I will
fulfill all My will concerning you. I will give you
mercies, holy and just things, as I did My servant David. Only believe, for My hand is upon
you. Wax bold. There are no limits set upon you
except the limits you set upon yourself. I am
shaping you to allow you passage through that
narrow doorway. Be patient, for once I have begun a good work in you, I will finish it. Just
trust Me, and allow Me. (Read Psalm 97:12 and
Matthew 7:14.)

February 21

◇

Self

**For he who has entered His rest has himself also
ceased from his works as God did from His. Let
us therefore be diligent to enter that rest, lest
anyone fall according to the same example
of disobedience (Hebrews 4:10–11).**

♦

*O Lord, when will I ever finish this difficult task?
Help my motives and intents to be right.*

The way before you is clear and uncluttered,
dear one. Only self can get in your way. With
great ease humanity allows petty grievance and
unproductive thinking to fog the windows of
the soul, so that it does not receive the only life
there is: My life-giving light. And in your case,
not all the evil powers of hell can hinder My divine power, but *you can*. Again I say, when you
allow yourself to be moved by anxiety or fear,
suspicion or unrest, you are opening a door
through which your keenly alert enemy may
shoot his fiery darts. Keep calm, unrushed, joy-
filled, loving . . . rested. (Read Ephesians 5:15–
17.)

◇

Confidence

Now this is the confidence that we have in Him, that if we ask anything according to His will, He hears us. And if we know that He hears us, whatever we ask, we know that we have the petitions that we have asked of Him (1 John 5:14–15).

♦

Lord, give me faith to believe You for a quick conclusion to this project.

Have confidence that I hear your cry and am answering. With the fullness of the Holy Spirit, you have power. Under the control of the Holy Spirit, you are enabled to live a fruitful life, like a tree firmly planted by streams of water which yields its fruit at the proper season. Claim abundant life and renewed strength as you wait for the finish of your work. And as you delight yourself in Me, I will give you the desire of your heart. To Jeremiah I said, "Call to Me, and I will answer you, and show you great and mighty things, which you do not know." It is faith which activates My promises. (Read Acts 19:2.)

Blessing or Disgrace?

**But you are not willing to come to Me that
you may have life (John 5:40).**

◆

*Though there has been great talk of Christianity,
so few nations or people have truly tried it; make me
a satisfactory Christian in Your sight, Lord.*

It is the only way to be spiritually alive: In
Me is life and that life is the light of men. Many
who are physically alive have no light in them.
But those who live according to the creator-
builder's directions operate at their fullest potential. When nations operate under My
principles, they are favored in the eyes of the
world, and disgraced when they walk in error. It
is the same for individuals: blessed or cursed.
The Bible is not open to diverse interpretations.
It is really very simple: Loving contact with My
Spirit makes one's life rich, abundant, overflowing, healthy, and filled with joy. Silent times
with Me make all the difference. And praise
profits much. (Read Deuteronomy 29:9.)

God's Faithfulness

But the Helper, the Holy Spirit, whom the
Father will send in My name, He will teach you
all things, and bring to your remembrance all
things that I said to you (John 14:26).

◆

*Thank You, Lord, that You are personal to me
and not an unknown God, that I can serve You with
knowledge and certainty, and not ignorance. For in
You we live, and move, and have our being.*

I am faithful. I reveal My secrets to those
who love Me and seek My perfect ways. They
are freely given by My Spirit who searches all
things, even My deep mysteries. Let there be no
division among you, but be perfectly adjusted
to each other, in the same mind and the same
judgment. Only then can you go forward to do
My appointed tasks without fear of con-
foundment, with strength and peace, and the
basic ingredient of ministry—love. Be not afraid.
Speak. Hold not your peace, for I am with you
to make you eloquent. (Read 1 Corinthians
2:7–12.)

◇

Fear

**And it shall come to pass that whoever calls
on the name of the LORD shall be
saved (Acts 2:21).**

◆

*Lord, I have awakened with fear in my heart
from a dream where I lost a loved one. What does it
mean, Lord? Is it from You? Or from the enemy to
destroy my sleep and instill fear?*

Fear is never from Me. Help is from Me. I
am your ever present help. Trust Me as you
would a faithful friend who you know would
come as promised. My Son, Jesus the Messiah,
saves from fear. Speak the name *Jesus* to every
doubt and worry, for He died to save you from
it. Every evil vanishes at that name, as the night
when the sun arises. Let your spirit rest now,
for no power can hinder My power. I speak long
life and happiness to you both. Trust Me. (Read
Psalm 23:4.)

Idolatry

**Since you have purified your souls in obeying
the truth through the Spirit in sincere love
of the brethren, love one another fervently
with a pure heart (1 Peter 1:22).**

◆

*O Lord, our deliverer, turn away ungodliness
from us; let not the spirit of competition and ambition
infiltrate Your work.*

Understand in depth what I am asking of
you. You have had opportunity for instruction,
and to whom much is given, much is required.
Walk orderly. Get quickly unentangled when
destructive, hellish spirits (selfish ambition or
competition, lying, aggravation, deception,
self-pity, jealousy, lust, fear) come and attempt
to destroy your joy and laughter and love. At
the first sign of unrest, drop everything and
hastily run to Me. Self is a trespass against love.
I warn you urgently—declare war on *all* selfishness, for what portion you keep, to that degree
you are faithless. Love gives. (Read Acts 22:14–
15 and 1 Corinthians 10:14.)

◇

Problems Solved

**Let this mind be in you which was also
in Christ Jesus (Philippians 2:5).**

◆

*Precious, majestic Lord of glory, who has known
Your Almighty mind? Thank You that You give us
the mind of Christ. Help us not to squander the privilege.*

Dear one, you have just spoken the formula
for making mountains move: the mind of
Christ, hearts of thanksgiving, and praiseful
worship. Oh, if My poor world only knew that
equation, all its problems would be solved in a
moment. But it is more than knowing, it is doing what the world considers foolishness. I appear to you so that you may speak and write,
warn and witness of those things you have seen
and those things I have yet to show you, so that
other eyes may be opened and turned from the
power of darkness to the Light. Be wise as a serpent and gentle as a dove, beloved. (Read Acts
26:16.)

Total Triumph

Elisha had become sick with the illness of which he would die. Then Joash the king of Israel came down to him, and wept over his face, and said, "O my father, my father, the chariots of Israel and their horsemen!" (2 Kings 13:14).

◆

Lord, I submit myself to You. I surrender all (insofar as I can read my heart). I resist the devil. Yet, I am not experiencing the glorious joy of a conquest won. What more would You have me do?

You need to declare war on hell. Remember, a roaring lion does not always roar to alert you. Stealthily he creeps up for the surprise attack, roaring only at that last moment. As My prophet Elisha said to King Joash, "You should have struck five or six times . . . But now you will strike Syria only three times." You gained the victory but not total triumph. Listen carefully to what I say: Storm the gates of hell, and the gates of hell will not prevail against you. March forth, confident of climactic and final triumph. (Read 2 Kings 13:14–19.)

February 29

◇

Live in the Belief

**Therefore submit to God. Resist the devil
and he will flee from you (James 4:7).**

◆

Excuse me, Lord . . .

*Satan, I rebuke you, fully resisting your sneaky
lying spirits that would attempt to infiltrate my
thoughts. I command you, in Jesus' name, to leave
these premises. You are the accuser. You shall not rule
in God's place.*

*Lord God, thank You for that power and author-
ity. For Your peace, for knowledge of Your Word and
principles. Thank You for this ultimate and eternal
union with You, Almighty One!*

Dear one, you are practicing what I have
taught you. Because you stand firm, you shall
not be moved. That is your victory through My
Son. I am building something in you that is going to last. (Read John 8:44 and Luke 1:45.)

March

A voice came out of the cloud,
saying, "This is My beloved
Son, in whom I am well
pleased. Hear Him!"

Matthew 17:5

March 1

◇

Submit Yourselves

**Bear one another's burdens, and so fulfill
the law of Christ (Galatians 6:2).**

◆

*Lord, stimulate me to the kind of simplicity that
breeds healthy growth, self-control, and comfortable-
ness.*

I will, so that you may correct and restore
those who are weak or failing in a spirit of gentleness. And in order for *you* to grow in love and
refinement of character, submit to others more
mature than yourself who are resources of My
collective wisdom. They will provide great safety
and help surface any residual bondage to past
hurt or failure. Avail yourself of therapeutic and
freeing ministry through these trustworthy leaders. At critical times of decision, personal weakness, bondage, or physical sickness, call for the
elders of the church, for effectual fervent prayer
is of much value. (Read Ephesians 4:1–2 and
James 5:13–16.)

◇

The Word and the Spirit

For He instructs him in right judgment, his God teaches him (Isaiah 28:26).

•

O Lord, our sure foundation, our precious corner-stone: Help me to be free of pride, whether it takes on the characteristics of unworthiness, lack of confidence, fear, or a puffed-up, "better-than" attitude. I throw myself on You, Lord.

I will instruct you in discretion, and teach you. I can only teach knowledge and understanding to those who are willing to be weaned from the breast and given solid food. My Word is solid: read it, hear it, honor it. It is strength and safety to you. Hear the Word of the Lord! This is the rest, the refreshing. Pray much for the Spirit of Holiness to resurrect that which is dead or dying in you, in your friends. My Spirit purges away the crown of pride, whose glorious beauty is a fading flower. I am your crown of glory, a diadem of lasting beauty. (Read Isaiah 28:9.)

March 3

◇

Trust and Obey

For what does the Scripture say? "Abraham believed God, and it was accounted to him for righteousness" (Romans 4:3).

◆

O Lord, let me be enlivened by the Holy Spirit; let no deceit be found in my tongue; cause my lips to be guileless—an antidote for the poison of the world; instead of bitter and critical, let my words be wise and edifying, peacemaking and courageous. And keep that healthy fear of You ever before my eyes.

Your prayer is being answered. Only believe. Abraham believed Me, and I counted it righteousness. Not because he did anything to earn it, otherwise the righteousness would have been a debt paid. But it was grace. Just as My grace forgives your iniquities and covers your sins, I reckon your faith for righteousness. Without faith you cannot please Me. Be more like My Son, your Messiah, in trust and obedience. My grace is abounding toward you. Sit and listen, believe and receive, and My Holy Spirit will deliver My messages. (Read Ephesians 2:8–10.)

All Empowerment

Therefore, as the elect of God, holy and beloved, put on tender mercies, kindness, humility, meekness, longsuffering (Colossians 3:12).

◆

Dear Lord, I pray for a heart of compassion. Teach me to sparkle in yearning intercession and sensitive supplication for the sick, sorrowful, and lost.

If you would be filled with compassion and prayer power, keep yourself in the sunshine of My love. Let not the clouds of doubt discourage you, nor time be frittered away with secondary things, nor conversation be wasteful, nor your stamina be exhausted, nor your thoughts swept away by petty, insignificant things. Be quickened by My Holy Spirit: All empowerment is available to make you fully faithful to your opportunities. When I tell you to do a certain thing, you must give it first priority. Develop a ravenous appetite for doing the little things and I will make you able to accomplish great things. (Read Colossians 3:12–17 and Matthew 25:23.)

◇

Nourishment

And he shall be like the light of the morning when the sun rises, a morning without clouds, like the tender grass springing out of the earth, by clear shining after rain (2 Samuel 23:4).

◆

O Lord, our great light, thank You for being as the tender grass springing out of the earth after rain.

Yes, I am all things to those who love Me, your all-sufficient nourishment. As My hungry lambs feed on Me and partake of My living Word, they are satisfied. Let My gentle spring breeze blow away the stale air of past orders and assignments. Receive "spring-clean" excitement and joy to go forward with the new tasks I give. I have uniquely equipped you with a compassionate and tender heart . . . take care that your strengths do not become your weaknesses. (Read Psalm 27:1.)

Intercession

If My people who are called by My name will humble themselves, and pray and seek My face, and turn from their wicked ways, then I will hear from heaven, and will forgive their sin and heal their land (2 Chronicles 7:14).

◆

O God, thank You for the opportunity to stand in the gap between this beloved country and You. Forgive us our selfishness, pride, and perversion. Bless the seat of our government with Your wisdom, Father, and cause those whom we have elected to be moral and godly, our Supreme Court to rely on the Supreme Power of the universe for the administration of justice.

The fervent prayer of a righteous woman or man is of much worth. I have heard your prayer, and I have recorded it. Some hearts do not listen, for their ears are hard of hearing. When that sound barrier is broken with prayer, gradually life will come. Pray *against* the spirits of humanism, idolatry, fear, and lust for power, and pray *for* leaders to be without partiality and without hypocrisy. (Read 1 Peter 4:7–8.)

◇

I Change Not

Knowing this, that our old man was crucified with Him, that the body of sin might be done away with, that we should no longer be slaves of sin. For he who has died has been freed from sin (Romans 6:6–7).

◆

Thank You, Lord, that You change not. There are so many facets to Your wondrous character that some might think You change as the seasons. But the basic law for the seasons also does not change. Although You asked Your disciples to take up their crosses, You also smiled at them as You prepared the lakeside feast; and probably laughed and had a good time at the marriage feast of Cana. Yet You wept over Jerusalem. The same . . . who changes not.

You can bury self with One who changes not. When you are crucified with Me, you shall be free. Humanity was programmed for wholeness, and the totality of My Word points you in the direction of ultimate satisfaction, fulfillment, creativity, and perfect order of body, mind, and spirit . . . life! (Read Hebrews 13:8.)

Power and Privilege

**For they being ignorant of God's righteousness,
and seeking to establish their own righteousness,
have not submitted to the righteousness
of God (Romans 10:3).**

◆

*Lord, keep us from seeking that independent style
of life and thought sanctified by the Renaissance man,
ignorant of You.*

Denial of My authority is the root of chaos
in the world and the root of unrest in individuals. When every man does that which is right in
his own eyes, spiritual vision is forfeited—as well
as the freedom of others—and man is tossed and
manipulated. It is a system of weakness and
foolishness, while Mine is a system of power and
wisdom. Direct access to Me through your Messiah does not render you invulnerable to error;
but by loving, trusting fellowship with Me, you
avoid games of mind control and counterfeit
spirituality. Test the spirits! As a citizen of My
Kingdom, be diligent in partaking of its privileges and disciplines. (Read Isaiah 1:19.)

◇

Honesty

**The secret of the LORD is with those who
fear Him, and He will show them
His covenant (Psalm 25:14).**

♦

*Oh, the depth of the riches of Your wisdom and
knowledge, O God, and Your ways past finding out!
Help me to understand; and surprise me by delivering
me from my conceits.*

Little by little, I am revealing to you My secrets, as you can receive them. When I say that
one gentle, loving, selfless word is of more importance to Me than a ruler's speech, believe
Me, for it is true. Only truth and life are valuable, and the honest humility of your life determines the degree of your value. Reverence Me.
It is the secret of learning My secrets. Be transformed by the renewing of your mind; think not
more highly of yourself than you ought; think
soberly according to your measure of faith. And
trust Me. (Read Romans 12:2–3.)

A New Creature

And now, Israel, what does the LORD your God require of you, but to fear the LORD your God, to walk in all His ways and to love Him, to serve the LORD your God with all your heart and with all your soul (Deuteronomy 10:12).

◆

Lord, sometimes I wish I could start all over again. Thank You for not casting us aside when we fail . . . for not being like us. Thank You for loving us enough to send Your Son, for not taking the easy way out and creating something new instead of redeeming. Make us more like You.

Let your faith and thankfulness result in praise and glory and honor at My revelation that you are a new creature. Believe it! Then love Me with your whole mind, heart, soul, and strength . . . and you will be able to love your fellow beings without guile, criticism, or prejudice. Gird your mind for action, keep sober in spirit, and fix your hope completely on the grace coming to you. Rejoice that I am making you more like Me. (Read 2 Corinthians 5:17.)

March 11

◇

Love

Let love be without hypocrisy. Abhor what is evil. Cling to what is good (Romans 12:9).

◆

Lord, help us to give liberally, speak Your truth diligently, show mercy and compassion cheerfully, and not be slothful in the running of our affairs.

My child, love is always appropriate. Tribute, custom, honor will not interfere nor cause discomfort when the simplicity of love is manifest. Love is the armor that casts off fear and other works of darkness. Love leaves no room for dishonesty, sloth, conceit, envy or strife, for love is comfortable being itself! Love stimulates peaceableness in one's nature, and peace abounds in hope. Pray for more empowerment through the Holy Ghost. (Read 1 Corinthians 13.)

Beauty of My Creation

The heavens declare the glory of God; and the firmament shows His handiwork (Psalm 19:1).

•

Ah, the brightness of Your glory, Lord, encompasses us. Your magnificence is in every bud of the peach tree, the smell of the orange blossoms, the white plum, and the liquid freshness of the roses as they bound back after pruning. How magnificent is Your new life this season of Your resurrection! Help us to take the time to absorb each of Your great thoughts abundantly manifest in the world.

O children, yes, let My beauty be so impressed upon your souls that it reflects in your actions, words, and thoughts. Draw hungering breaths of fresh, pure air. Bask in the sunlight of My love. Seek My silence. Be transformed now (physically, mentally, spiritually) for the season of dryness is over. Even on My Son's way to the cross, the scorn and suffering did not prevent Him from seeing the beauty of My creation. Hear Me! Let nothing stop your appreciation, your loving, your laughter! (Read Psalm 72:19.)

Overcoming

**For the kingdom of God is not in word
but in power (1 Corinthians 4:20).**

♦

*Lord, for some reason I feel like an offscouring to-
day. Perhaps it comes from the dream I awoke with,
the knot in my stomach, or the lack of confidence in
my ability to do what needs to be done today. Whatever the reason, I feel like I need to be loved.*

A gray day is a day for thankfulness. Think
of My character on days such as this, and be not
puffed up with pride, as though I would not
come to you. The Kingdom of God is not just
in Word but in power. All power is Mine: to
heal, to deliver, to bind up, to loose, to restore
everything the cankerworm has eaten, to lift
your head when you feel like an offscouring. I
love you. And all things really do work together
for good for them that love Me. Give Me the
moments today, My child; give Me all your
love. Let praise be at the core of your being, for
I inhabit the praise of My people . . . and you
shall be lifted up. (Read Romans 8:28.)

Seek Me First

Nevertheless I have this against you, that you have left your first love (Revelation 2:4).

•

Lord, how is it that so many churches are dying, their people knowing Your Word and honoring You with their lips, but without power?

They are wise in their own eyes. Having lost their first love (the love of Christ), they believe that their strivings for a good cause will merit My blessing. Seek My Kingdom first, and all these things—funds, buildings, deliverances, healings—will be the result. My ways are ever fresh, ever new, ever fruitful; man's ways are ever stale, ever dying, eternally unproductive. I know the thoughts of humanity, that they are vain, glorying in other men and their opinions. To experience power, the church must be willing to give up herself and her ministries, and give Me back the gifts I've given, with all humility, sincerity of heart, integrity, and truth. I am the receptacle of all power, faith, love, creativity, and ability. (Read 2 Timothy 3:5.)

March 15

◇

Responsibility

**But as God has distributed to each one, as the
Lord has called each one, so let him walk.
And so I ordain in all the churches
(1 Corinthians 7:17).**

◆

*Lord, as You have called me, so let me walk—not
evaluating or trying to attain someone else's spirituality, but strictly adhering to Your commands to me: to
abide in You, to take authority over my own will, to be
strong in conscience, and to eagerly embrace my cross.*

You have what you ask. I know you. I recognize your love for Me. In receiving knowledge
or glory, dear one, remember never to be puffed
up by it. Take heed also that your liberty or understanding not be a hindrance to one who is
weak in faith or mind; take care never to wound
another's conscience or to cause a withering in
his spirit. Yes, eagerly embrace your cross, for on
it the self that hinders your growth and prevents
you from hearing My voice will be crucified.
Follow Me daily—rejoicing, loving, and laugh-
ing as you go. (Read 1 Corinthians 8:2, 9.)

◇

Judging Separates

**For if we would judge ourselves, we would
not be judged (1 Corinthians 11:31).**

◆

*Give me the courage to judge myself, Lord, so that
You won't have to. And let me not judge or criticize
others, but have the inner disposition to go with them
to their weak, vulnerable, lonely, and broken places.*

To enter into compassionate solidarity with
those who suffer, you must first give up measuring your meaning and value by another's yard-
stick. When you cease to evaluate others, then
you stop comparing yourself, thereby freeing
yourself to be compassionate. Judging separates.
When you put people into categories of good,
bad, or indifferent, it influences your own
thoughts, words, and actions toward them. Humanity is limited by the entrapments of its own
judgments. If only you would take the log from
your own eye before trying to take the speck
from others'. It takes a death to be raised up. It
takes humbling to be exalted. It takes giving up
to be able to have. (Read Matthew 7:1.)

Love

**[Love] bears all things, believes all things,
hopes all things, endures all things
(1 Corinthians 13:7).**

◆

*Dear loving Father, You have told us to have large
visions, that nothing is too big: I claim love, for all
those You love . . . all, Lord. Earnest—in season and
out of season, caring, instant, good-Samaritan love
which stops to help in the midst of disaster—not considering itself but others.*

Beloved, you have asked for the greatest gift.
Prayer, teaching, sacrifice, knowledge, service,
amount to nothing if not joined with love. I am
love. Without Me, the idea of love is an exercise
of self aimed to attract flattering comment or
make one's sense of right and wrong register
points. When a soul born into My Kingdom enters the fulfilling life eternal (knowing Me), then
real love begins to be experienced and passed on.
Rest in, trust in My love until it becomes your
first response—true and spontaneous. (Read
1 Corinthians 13:1–7 and 1 John 4:7–8.)

Loving Service

Pursue love, and desire spiritual gifts,
but especially that you may prophesy
(1 Corinthians 14:1).

◆

*Thank You, Father, that You speak to us, and
that we hear Your voice: by revelation, by knowledge,
by prophecy, and by doctrine. How You build us up,
stir us up, and lift us up by speaking through Your
servants, and through us to others. Let us excel in
edifying. Help us to be as innocent as little children
when it comes to malice, but grown up in our understanding of love and service. Help us to be such fine
examples of Your life that unbelievers will be convinced of Your existence.*

I speak clearly. I am not the author of confusion but of peace, and I give you the ability to
be loving in all that you do. Die daily, that you
may more freely build up, exhort, and comfort
My church. Be not deceived. *Any* evil corrupts.
All good is incorruptible. Be selfless, loving,
serving, refreshed in your spirit by My Spirit.
(Read 1 Corinthians 14:3–6.)

March 19

◇

Door of Opportunity

**For a great and effective door has opened
to me, and there are many adversaries
(1 Corinthians 16:9).**

♦

*Lord, You have said You would do new and
mighty things through us, that the anointing of the
past would be as nothing compared to the anointing
to come, that a door would open where there is no door.
When, Lord?*

The significance of an open door is the provision of opportunity. The door is opened by
obedience and faith. But the only One with authority to grant access is the exalted Christ. Listen once again: *Praises, worship, and thanksgiving
are the paths of entry into My presence.* Obedience
brings you to the throne room, faith protects
you, the armor of light deflects the evil. But for
every door, there are many adversaries waiting to
divert you and keep you from entering. On
guard! Watch! Pray without ceasing. Guard
your thoughts that you be not distracted. (Read
Psalm 22:3.)

Ever-Present Help

Blessed be the God and Father of our Lord Jesus Christ, the Father of mercies and God of all comfort (2 Corinthians 1:3).

◆

Father of mercies and God of all comfort, I offer myself afresh for You to pour Your love through to those in any sort of trouble. Come, glorious Lord, unfold Your promises upon us this day.

I am your ever-present help. But to the degree that you trust in yourself and your own wisdom, that help does not operate, nor godly wisdom flourish. When your child says, "I will do it," then access to your greater knowledge is not allowed. But when that same one comes with outstretched hands, the broken toy—or emotions—held out for you to fix, your wisdom and experience freely go to work. You are blessed that your child believes in you, trusts you, and comes to you. So it is with Me. By faith you stand. It is your choice to invite Me in or leave Me out. Never have I failed you! I give you grace, great grace. (Read 2 Corinthians 1:3–5.)

◇

Go Forward Unafraid

Therefore you shall be perfect, just as your Father in heaven is perfect (Matthew 5:48).

◆

Why do I rush so, hurrying my life away? Lord, show me daily what I must do!

Keep your heart with all diligence, for out of it flow the springs of life. Put far from you pointless and perverse speech. Let your eyes look straight ahead. Go forward unafraid . . . that is your direction! Forget the past, stretch out beyond your capacity, reach toward the high calling to which I have called you. Strive for mastery and perfection. Have a single eye toward Me. Let there be no darkness in you. Illuminate the place in which you work, stand, and walk. Do not feel that I have called you to something unattainable, for I make all things possible. It is not through your rushing, striving busyness that it is possible but through My power . . . and your availability. (Read Proverbs 4:20–27; Philippians 3:13–14.)

Obedience

**And He said to them, "Why did you seek Me?
Did you not know that I must be about
My Father's business?" (Luke 2:49).**

♦

*Show me how You made it through the world,
Lord Jesus, with absolute grace and poise and perfection, that I may follow You.*

The absolute and unavoidable was made
simple for Me because I allowed *no doubt* about
doing what My Father said I must do: suffer
many things, be about My Father's business,
serve, preach the Kingdom of God, keep going,
have relationships, die to all of Myself, work
while the opportunity and freedom were available. All . . . that the Father be glorified. This
is the way of grace and poise and perfection. It
is easy and the workload is light when you do
not hesitate to do what the Father tells you.
Trust Me. I will help you. (Read 2 Thessalonians
2:13–14; Mark 8:31; Luke 4:43; 13:33; John
3:14–15; 9:4.)

◇

Restoration

Furthermore, we have had human fathers who corrected us, and we paid them respect. Shall we not much more readily be in subjection to the Father of spirits and live? (Hebrews 12:9).

◆

Forgive me, Lord, for omitting the truth. You who are my stamina and encouragement, preserve in me the integrity of Your faultless being: perfectly dependable, completely consistent, and absolutely truthful. You cannot be less than Yourself . . . help me not to be less than myself.

My child, your salvation is an ongoing attribute of Myself through My Son as Savior, My Word as truth, and My Spirit as sanctifier. I call you to continued growth in the likeness of My Son—perfectly holy—and a complete submission of your human imperfection to Me for total restoration. I will deal with you in a consistent, balanced manner—confronting, releasing . . . making you more of the unique and wondrous personality I created you to be. (Read Hebrews 12:10.)

Perfection

**Therefore, leaving the discussion of the
elementary principles of Christ, let us go on to
perfection, not laying again the foundation of
repentance from dead works and of faith
toward God (Hebrews 6:1).**

◆

*Lord, show me how to reduce the scope of my life,
narrowing the funnel to increase the force.*

Living close to holy things, working in the
church, even speaking holy things does not nec-
essarily mean one is living a holy life. Excellence
in faith, knowledge, endurance, patience, or
endless love requires the habit of discipline.
Habit means exercise . . . a maturing process.
Just as a beginning apple is perfect, you can be
perfect for your stage of development. An ongoing maturity is very simple: Think on things
that are true, honest, just, pure, lovely, of good
report. If there be any virtue or anything to
praise, think on these. Follow Me. Those things
you have seen Me do, you do! And My peace
shall be with you. (Read Matthew 7:14.)

Enablement

Not that we are sufficient of ourselves to think of anything as being from ourselves, but our sufficiency is from God (2 Corinthians 3:5).

◆

Lord, Your strength, Your courage, Your faith, Your persistence, and Your boldness are needed for the week ahead. Through Your intervention alone can I get through it.

Where the Spirit of the Lord is, there is liberty. Welcome My Holy Spirit to bring all you need for the week ahead, including My messages, and you will be changed. Don't block My way, and watch Me do the work. Your sufficiency is in Me. You have renounced the hidden things of dishonesty. Now, allow My full light to shine . . . to give you knowledge and excellence and power for the task before you. Die to your own desire, that My desire may be manifest and resurrected in you, renewing you day by day. This light affliction is accomplishing a far-reaching and eternal weight of glory. I love you with all My heart. (Read 2 Corinthians 3:17.)

Deliverance

And the Lord will deliver me from every evil work and preserve me for His heavenly kingdom. To Him be glory forever and ever. Amen! (2 Timothy 4:18).

♦

Dear Lord, I pray that Your voice be the One we hear today, and not the voice of man, nor the voice of the enemy. As the placenta cocoons, insulates, and nourishes the fetus, surround us with Yourself.

As My servants draw on My nourishment, they are called to serve the Good News to the world. Available and filled up with My love and givingness, your ministry gift, talent, time, and financial resources may be used to save and release this generation. Today is the acceptable time: Receive My enablement; grow in compassion and commitment; be balanced and sensitive; reach out to My poor world and snatch those barren, anguished lives out of the hands of Satan. I am your deliverer. I am your protector. My compassions are new every morning. (Read 2 Timothy 4:17.)

◇

Abundance

Now I rejoice, not that you were made sorry,
but that your sorrow led to repentance. For you
were made sorry in a godly manner, that you
might suffer loss from us in nothing
(2 Corinthians 7:9).

◆

*When I first came to You, Lord of glory, my flesh
had no rest, and there was guile and masking on every
side: without was fighting and struggle; within was
fear. But You lifted my head and gave me an earnest
desire to serve You. I will never cease to love You, and
I will praise You, majestic Lord, all of my life.*

To whom much is forgiven, that one loves
much. Sorrow for sin works carefulness, and a
clearing of self, resentment, fear, and passionate
need, which allows you to abound in everything—faith, speech, heavenly language and
knowledge, diligence and discipline, and your
love for Me. Openness begets openness. Make
yourself vulnerable to greater grace. (Read 2 Corinthians 7:10.)

Giving

So let each one give as he purposes in his heart, not grudgingly or of necessity; for God loves a cheerful giver (2 Corinthians 9:7).

◆

Help us to stand, O Lord, in a stance conducive to maturity, remembering always that giving will free, and keeping will cost.

Unselfish giving is cheerful, and I do love a cheerful giver. I will stir you to give, and when you obey, see if I do not open the windows of heaven and pour out blessings so great that there will not be room enough to contain it. Also, I will rebuke the devourer for your sakes. He shall not destroy the fruits of your labor. You shall not lose what is meant for you. And you shall receive a hundredfold *now,* in this time. With the same measuring cup you give out, it will be measured to you. It is a principle of giving—whether self or money. (Read Luke 6:38 and Mark 10:30.)

March 29

◇

Guard Your Thoughts

**Beware, brethren, lest there be in any of you
an evil heart of unbelief in departing from
the living God (Hebrews 3:12).**

◆

*Give us spiritual eyes, Bright and Morning Star,
to awaken us, to recognize our enemy's tactics . . .*

First, you must attack fear as you would a
snake or scorpion or great poisonous spider trying to enter your house. Cast out every imagination—every device that tries to exalt itself or cast
doubt on My loving hopes and peaceful desires
for your life, or on My ability to answer your
prayers. Bring every thought obediently back to
Me, thinking only that which is pure and loving, forgiving and faith provoking. Use My
Word, for it is a two-edged sword. Be simple!
For simplicity is a clear window, whereas com-
plexity's very nature is confusing. There is also
power in rest. I communicate more easily
through a vessel whose mind is at peace. Remember that Satan attacks the weak and belea-
guered. (Read Luke 10:19.)

Faith

Therefore know that only those who are of faith are sons of Abraham (Galatians 3:7).

◆

Omniscient and omnipotent Lord, by Your awesome creativity let Your life-creating words create greater faith in us.

They which are of faith, the same are the children of Abraham. I promised Abraham that in him all nations would be blessed. Your faith makes you blessed by that promise . . . you can be a blesser of men and nations. If only My people will believe and doubt not, they can have what they say. To believe one must relinquish pride. The seed—to live and be fruitful—must break open in the soil. When it dies, it allows fresh new life to spring forth with greater potential for seed bearing, therefore greater creativity than ever before. Learn from this. (Read Romans 4:20–21.)

March 31

◇

Loyalty

Let the heavens rejoice, and let the earth be glad; and let them say among the nations, "The LORD reigns" (1 Chronicles 16:31).

◆

Great Captain of the army of the Lord, give us the victory—over our critical flesh, our self, wanting its own way, our enemy, who uses it all for his honor. As You were totally loyal to the Father's purpose when You took authority over Your suffering and chose the Cross, inspire in us that same totality of trust, that complete loyalty to You and Your will.

The victory is nigh. Each week is one of steady progress. You may not see it now, but in retrospect, you will. Though you may see your work as slow and plodding, I see the progress of your heart. Your greatest weapons are thankfulness and joy, worship and praise, love and laughter. I know how you function best. I created the cells of your body. And when My Holy Spirit passes through My sons and daughters, He imparts knowledge of Me, loyalty to Me, loyalty to My body. (1 Chronicles 16:27–35.)

April

Incline your ear, and come
to Me. Hear, and your
soul shall live.

Isaiah 55:3

April 1

◇

Victorious Life

The sting of death is sin, and the strength of sin is the law (1 Corinthians 15:56).

◆

O Lord, my Lord, my sins have injured You just as surely as those who pinned You to the cross.

This Easter season is the most wondrous time of all time. And were it not for the resurrection, you would surely be doomed! But rejoice! If there was ever a time to be glad it is now. No mournful, long face at My crucifixion—although there is a time to identify with My suffering. Put on the face of risen life and take off those grave clothes. I have a wonderful blessing for you—yes, a breakthrough of triumph and release. Fling your arms wide in loving expectation and invitation. Lay down your wishes and desires, lay down your past and future, lay down your cares, lay down your life! And I will give you a richer, more dynamic life than you can imagine. (Read 1 Corinthians 15:54–58.)

Protection

**Then Jesus said to him, "Away with you, Satan!
For it is written, 'You shall worship the LORD
your God, and Him only you shall serve.'"
Then the devil left Him (Matthew 4:10–11).**

◆

*Thank You, Lord, that You've called me to
"watch" with You. I serve only You.*

As the palm frond at the center stands fully
upright while all those surrounding it are blown
and tossed and torn by the winds, so it is with
you when you are in the *center* of My will—fully
protected, unmovable, always upright . . . and
the angels surround you to do battle, to protect,
and even to take the blows for you. (Read Isaiah
54:17.)

April 3

◇

Rest

**So why do you worry about clothing? Consider
the lilies of the field, how they grow: they
neither toil nor spin (Matthew 6:28).**

◆

*Father, thank You for treating me as Your full-
fledged child and not as a reject, which I deserve.*

I have no stepchildren and no grandchildren. Only children. Just as the bird is comfortable in the air—whether the air is calm and
peaceful or turbulent with skies raining around
it—so it is for you, My child, to be comfortable
and "at home" in My presence. Never strug-
gling or striving. Silent. Peaceful. Unpressed.
Dependent on Me, you will reach your goal.
(Read Philippians 4:4–7.)

Peace

But God, who is rich in mercy, because of His great love with which He loved us, even when we were dead in trespasses, made us alive together with Christ (by grace you have been saved) (Ephesians 2:4–5).

◆

O Great Master, our guide, thank You for shining Your mighty searchlight upon Satan that we might see his true image, recognize and hate his acts, and deny him entry.

Even before your obedience to Me, My child, was I rich in mercy toward you and healed you. Even when you were dead in sin did I give you a measure of faith. I created man for good, to be holy as I am holy, perfect, and lacking nothing. I am your peace. I made peace; I preached peace. Receive My peace, by My Spirit. Look for it nowhere beside. You were made a perfect receptacle, built as a holy temple for My Holy Spirit. I inhabit your praise. Raise your hands and make a joyful sound. (Read Ephesians 2:17–18.)

April 5

Selflessness

**Then Jesus said to His disciples, "If anyone
desires to come after Me, let him deny himself,
and take up his cross, and follow Me. For
whoever desires to save his life will lose it,
but whoever loses his life for My sake
will find it" (Matthew 16:24–25).**

◆

*Lord, replace my self-consciousness with conscious-
ness of You.*

There is no place for Me in a person who is
filled up with self. But as you spend time with
Me, I crowd self out. When you give up your
own motives and inclinations, you make room
for Me. Flesh becomes like the "god" it serves.
All who honestly seek Me will find Me. I am
here. (Read Philippians 2:5.)

Holiness

**But you are not willing to come to Me
that you may have life (John 5:40).**

◆

Make me whole, O Holy One!

It is not the sun that creates the shadows,
but that thing that obstructs the sun. So it is
with dark and hidden things in one's personality
that stand between that one and the Son . . .
hindering, casting shadows on the entire person. That first Easter, My broken body was
raised that you might be put back together . . .
whole, holy, lacking nothing. Receive wholeness—body, mind, emotions, and spirit. I gave
My life's blood that you might have life and
have it more abundantly. Take life. Take forgiveness. I bless your life. You bless Me, too, as you
trust and obey. (Read John 6:35.)

April 7

Healing

Brethren, I do not count myself to have apprehended; but one thing I do, forgetting those things which are behind and reaching forward to those things which are ahead, I press toward the goal for the prize of the upward call of God in Christ Jesus (Philippians 3:13–14).

Lord, deliver me from the past.

Just as a cat running after a bird gets thorns in its feet along the cactus-ridden desert, you have picked up things that would prick and sting along your path, as you ran after elusive pursuits. Hold those areas out to Me and I will remove the thorns, for I, of all, know how they pierce the flesh and soul and weigh down the spirit. Once removed, these thorns lose their ability to wound. Depend on Me and the surgery will be easy. Reach out to those good things before you. (Read Song of Solomon 2:10–11.)

Calm Is Constructive

**Also it is not good for a soul to be without
knowledge, and he sins who hastens
with his feet (Proverbs 19:2).**

◆

Lord, I know You want me to rest—not fearing.

The world moves swiftly toward success, but
you to achieve must learn to be calm. All rush,
all stress, all agitation is destructive. My peace is
constructive, destroying disease and evil. As you
rest in Me, change and growth will come as easily as walking from one room to another, and
just as comfortably. Continue to keep these
times with Me, where we speak heart to heart,
sharing our deepest concerns. You will never
know, this side of heaven, the inroads made into
the kingdom of darkness, the dispersing of pollution in the world, the growth and power
loosed in your own life and those for whom you
pray. Peace, peace, peace! Let not your spirit be
moved, except by Me. Resist not My calming
presence. (Read Psalm 37:7.)

April 9

◇

Abundant Life

**Arise, shine; for your light has come!
And the glory of the LORD is risen
upon you (Isaiah 60:1).**

◆

Thank You, Lord, for being alive.

Arise and shine . . . arise and shine, My children, for your light is come, and the glory of the Lord is risen upon you. I call you from death to life. Be resurrected from fear and despair, from sickness, distrust, criticism, and contention. I call you to believe in Me, to have hope, to give love, joy and health and peace. Allow Me to fill the emptiness in your bosom. Let My glory fall upon you and surround you as the air you breathe. Let My Holy Spirit fill you as the blood that courses through your veins, that if any part of you be pricked, I would come forth. I came that you might have rich, abundant life. Claim it this morning, for it is time. (Read John 10:10.)

A Day for Healing

Let us therefore come boldly to the throne of grace, that we may obtain mercy and find grace to help in time of need (Hebrews 4:16).

♦

Lord, give us courage to face this new day. All our plans seem to be falling apart.

O My children, come before Me with boldness and thanksgiving, content with what I am about to do. Arise and shine! This is the day that I have made . . . a day for you to bring your broken hearts to be mended; your fears to be exchanged for courage; your infirmities to be healed. Bring Me your cares and worries and woes . . . I want to soothe and free you. I am a God of love and mercy. (Read Luke 4:18.)

Discipline

For they indeed for a few days chastened us as seemed best to them, but He for our profit, that we may be partakers of His holiness. Now no chastening seems to be joyful for the present, but painful; nevertheless, afterward it yields the peaceable fruit of righteousness to those who have been trained by it (Hebrews 12:10–11).

◆

Help me, Lord, to walk softly before You.

Learn to love discipline. Train yourself to obedience. Discipline will remove the mountains which you desire to be gone from your life. Be strong and firm with yourself. And don't give up one point that you have gained. You are constantly moving. If you are not moving forward, you are going backward, never just standing in place. Do not retreat but go forward unafraid. *Unafraid*. Discipline yields righteousness. Righteous discipline yields holiness. (Read Joshua 1:7.)

◇

Faithfulness

Therefore gird up the loins of your mind, be sober, and rest your hope fully upon the grace that is to be brought to you at the revelation of Jesus Christ (1 Peter 1:13).

♦

Thank You, Lord, for Your faithfulness.

My glory follows them that follow Me. Those who gird up the loins of their minds and are sober and hope to the end for grace through Jesus Christ shall not be confounded. I will *never* fail. I will live and abide and be faithful forever with those who have purified souls (minds and emotions), who are born spiritually and love one another fervently. Sanctify Me in your heart, and be ready always to give an answer to those who ask you the reason for the hope they see in you. (Read 1 Peter 3:15.)

◇

Your Finest Hour

**. . . giving thanks always for all things to
God the Father in the name of our
Lord Jesus Christ (Ephesians 5:20).**

◆

*Dear Lord, it seems as if the days are impossibly
short to perform all the tasks: menial and exalted,
necessary and expected, requested and invited. How do
we decide which things to do and which to leave?*

Your most important hour of the day is
here . . . it is a base for everything else. This hour
with Me is the sunlight that shines upon the rest
of your day. From here, walk the path of pro-
ductivity, with all sincerity. Speak to yourself in
psalms and hymns and spiritual songs, making
melody in your heart. Pray readily and easily for
those in your way. That is the only way that
writing, cleaning, shopping, helping, speaking,
visiting, or studying can all be done with ease.
To the degree that self is tolerated man is unable
to cope. Leave no doors open for hell to enter.
Receive peace . . . and you will make right decisions. (Read Ephesians 5:18–20.)

Arm Yourself

But Jesus looked at them and said to them, "With men this is impossible, but with God all things are possible" (Matthew 19:26).

◆

Dear Lord, strengthen us that we may be able to stand patiently against the evil of these days.

Put on My whole armor, My children: the garment of praise, against a spirit of heaviness and the chafe of the armor; the helmet of salvation; the breastplate of righteousness; gird yourself with truth; walk in the shoes of the preparation of the gospel of peace; carry the shield of faith to quench *all* the fiery darts of the enemy; the sword of the Spirit, which is My Word. Pray always in the Spirit. Watch with perseverance. Deal with the issues, not in your own strength but by My Spirit. When you ask what to do, I will tell you. Then expect things to change as I intervene. Act like things are changing. Do not speak your doubts. When you do all that you can do, then I will do the impossible. (Read Ephesians 6:11–18.)

April 15

◇

Vigilance

**. . . being confident of this very thing, that He
who has begun a good work in you will
complete it until the day of Jesus
Christ (Philippians 1:6).**

◆

*Please, Lord, continue the good work You have
begun in us.*

I will perform it until the day My Son returns. Never give up a single principle learned,
nor allow to slide a place you've conquered. Ap-
prove things that are excellent, not lending your
name to anything shoddy, petty, or without
merit. Be honest in love and joy, without falsity
or hilarity. Let My mind be in you. Strive not
for a reputation—and never give yourself credit
for what is My doing. As you look to Me, I will
enable you to *want* and to *do* what is good and
right and profitable without murmuring or disputing. My admonition to you today is to open
your mouth with wisdom and let the law of
kindness be in your tongue. You will see why it
had to be. (Read Proverbs 31:26.)

The Mind of Christ

**And the peace of God, which surpasses all
understanding, will guard your hearts and
minds through Christ Jesus (Philippians 4:7).**

◆

*Dear Lord, You came to earth as a flesh-and-
blood man, lived as a man, did everything subject to
the same human limitations we have. Please, how
and where did You learn all You knew—scholarly
things to teach in the synagogue, all Scriptures, healing, deliverance? Not that I doubt Your Divinity, for
the Father could have taught You sovereignly as You
worked in the carpentry shop or in the fields, but. . . .*

I kept all of My Father's commandments;
therefore, sin was never present to clutter My
mind and emotions. I let My mind abide in the
Father, listening. Anxiety and fear hinder awareness. I had the peace of God. I thought only of
things that were true, honest, just, pure, lovely,
good and virtuous, and godly. Let My mind be
in you. Humble yourself. And this peace, and
My total awareness, will keep your heart and
mind. (Read Colossians 3:15.)

◇

Love

**But above all these things put on love, which is
the bond of perfection (Colossians 3:14).**

◆

*Sometimes I feel so inarticulate and intellectually
lean, Father. Fatten me up with understanding.*

Pray much for love . . . perfect love casts out
the fear which inhibits speech and self-control,
sound-mindedness, and power. When you love,
your mind is off yourself. (Read 1 Peter 4:8.)

Cleansing

But the fruit of the Spirit is love, joy, peace, longsuffering, kindness, goodness, faithfulness, gentleness, self-control. Against such there is no law (Galatians 5:22–23).

◆

Lord, forgive us for polluting this planet, this beautiful creation of Yours.

As the smog covers the valleys of the world, so it is a picture of how the world has tried to cover, submerge, hide, suppress the natural beauty of the Gospel and the purity of My love. Only through My followers can the wind of the Holy Spirit blow the pollution away and bring peace, love, joy, gentleness, goodness, meekness, faith, patience, and self-control to a suffering mankind. (Read Psalm 16:11.)

◇

Cheerful Obedience

Therefore, as the elect of God, holy and beloved, put on tender mercies, kindness, humility, meekness, longsuffering; bearing with one another, and forgiving one another, if anyone has a complaint against another; even as Christ forgave you, so you also must do (Colossians 3:12–13).

♦

O Father, do a fresh new thing in me today. Show me how to be "on duty," even when it's not convenient, with all joy and grace and poise.

As you attired yourself this morning for the day ahead, I say now: Put on mercy, patience, ease of forgiveness, and peaceableness. And whatever you do, do it heartily. (Read Isaiah 43:19.)

Nourishment

Now may the God of peace Himself sanctify you completely; and may your whole spirit, soul, and body be preserved blameless at the coming of our Lord Jesus Christ (1 Thessalonians 5:23).

◆

Lord, show us the perfect nutrients for our spirits, as You have for our bodies.

You know the fruits of My Holy Spirit; there are also vegetables: discipline, obedience, worship, prayer, service, and self-abandon—the staples of My Kingdom. It takes both fruit and vegetables to grow healthy and strong. Eat well from this garden and you will be strong in your spirit, soul (mind and emotions), and body. Leave something out and you will be malnourished. I want only what is profitable for you . . . and what is good for you is good for your family. (Read Genesis 50:21.)

April 21

◇

Prophecy

**Nor did we seek glory from men, either from
you or from others, when we might have made
demands as apostles of Christ. But we were
gentle among you, just as a nursing
mother cherishes her own children
(1 Thessalonians 2:6–7).**

◆

*Lord, Your Word tells us to seek to prophesy. I pray
for the trust and courage to give prophecy.*

I will give you prophecy. I will anoint you.
Search your conscience for deceit so that you
speak no flattering words nor use Me as a cloak
for your motives. I am your witness! Seek not
your own glory! Be gentle, even as a mother to
her children—affectionate, loving, desiring only
to impart that which I speak (not embellishing
nor ornamenting, not caring whether it is one
word or a volume). You do not have to labor
and travail, but boldly speak what I say; encour-
age, comfort, and charge My people to follow
Me, unceasingly, thankfully. (Read 1 Corinthians 14:3–5 and 1 Thessalonians 2:3–7.)

Spiritual Resources

But the Helper, the Holy Spirit, whom the Father will send in My name, He will teach you all things, and bring to your remembrance all things that I said to you (John 14:26).

◆

Thank You for calling me to "watch" with You. Why, when You could summon all the angels to Your defense, did You keep going back to Peter, James, and John and wanting them to watch with You?

Have you never considered that it was My human loneliness crying out for the warm love and understanding of My brothers, even though they did not understand? If they had known and believed it was My very last night, they would have stayed awake with Me, but the Spirit of Truth had not yet come to show them the things to come . . . that same Spirit of Truth which reveals to you today what the Father says. You have learned more truth since you have given yourself over to My Lordship than in all the previous years. Think on this! (Read Matthew 26:38–41.)

Perfection

**For you know what commandments we gave you through the Lord Jesus. For this is the will of God, your sanctification: that you should abstain from sexual immorality
(1 Thessalonians 4:2–3).**

◆

Show me what I must do, Lord, after I have done all I know, to be constant in goodness, perfect in obedience, and complete in love.

It is My will that you be pure and holy, without criticism, loving one another always. How good it is for the soul, without restlessness and anxiety, to link all thoughts to Me. I lack nothing. I am entirely sufficient. I am holy. I am the totality of creation and creativity. I am your source for: protection, stamina, growth, guidance, authority, comfort, reality, forgiveness, provision, boldness, restraint, loveliness, confidence, defense, purpose, freedom, awakening, and victory . . . whatever you need. (Read Hebrews 4:9–10 and Leviticus 20:7–8.)

Love

**By your patience possess your
souls (Luke 21:19).**

◆

Lord, show me how to love as You love.

Prepare yourself for the allowance of love: Be diligent in these times of communion with Me, diligent in waiting. Put on the breastplate of faith, which acts as a shield against your enemy, guarding your heart. Be free in My presence, never covering up, manipulating, or presuming. Be watchful and sober. I enter through a door marked "Peace." Never allow agitation to take you for even a moment. It is a subtle agent for the destroyer. Practice being patient. Rejoice more, letting every hour of life and breath be a cause for it. Pray continually, always ready and available to My Spirit. Then you will more clearly love as I love. (Read 1 John 4:11–12.)

Obedience

**And we know that all things work together for
good to those who love God, to those who
are the called according to His
purpose (Romans 8:28).**

◆

*Dear Lord, this morning I awoke with an awful
foreboding, an oppression over what I cannot tell.*

Be honest! You will feel ashamed if you do
not yield to Me on this point. It is a question
of your will, not of debate or reasoning. The crisis is a matter of absolute and irrevocable surrender of yourself. Keeping you from deciding is
the over-consideration for your self and your
comfort, while you act as if it is your consider-
ation for others. Do you think I don't know the
cost of your obedience? I do know. Shut out
everything else and determine absolutely to do
My will. This crisis point came because you did
not heed My gentler way. It is a providential crisis. I will never hurt you or keep you from any
good thing. All things work together for your
good. Trust Me. (Read Philippians 2:13–14.)

Overcoming

**Yet in all these things we are more than
conquerors through Him who
loved us (Romans 8:37).**

♦

*Father! Help! My mind and emotions have been
trampled on as I slept, yet I know that You are the
lifter of my head.*

Because of My permanent and ongoing
promise, the intercession of My Son and the
Holy Spirit's power, you shall more than conquer; you shall do valiantly. Do not allow your
adversary, Satan, a moment's pleasure at your
intimidation. I am aligning you for a new assault
on the powers of darkness. March to My ca-
dence. Finely tune your ear to My commands.
That is the way you overcome! (Read Psalm
60:12.)

April 27

◇

Be Still

**Be still, and know that I am God; I will be
exalted among the nations, I will be
exalted in the earth! (Psalm 46:10).**

◆

Abba, Father, You are my hope and shield.

Be settled, as one in the act of being born.
Have an innate sense that says "all is well" while
the mechanism about you is doing the work. Be
still, and know that I am God. After this period
of stillness and labor you will be brought into
new life, refreshed, cleansed, and whole. You
will see that this period of incubation and this
time of drawing away with Me is essential. Only
when you come to be with Me will you fully
understand the power that becomes available
through these holy hours. I honor you with My
presence. (Read Psalm 139:14–18.)

Your Intimate Lord

You shall walk in all the ways which the LORD your God has commanded you, that you may live and that it may be well with you, and that you may prolong your days in the land which you shall possess (Deuteronomy 5:33).

◆

O Lord, help me to stop needing to be understood, identified with, or accepted. When will I enter that intimacy with You that precludes wanting my own way? Have an unhindered way in me, dear Jesus, and fill the last abyss of my personality with Yourself.

Your quest for a more intimate relationship with Me gives Me joy. If it were My choice, I would walk and communicate freely with you in the early morning and the cool of the evening. But it is you who choose the time. I come . . . your intimate Lord . . . and I impress upon you a stronger, calmer sanity, greater ability to love, purer heart, and clearer conscience. Unpretending and unpretentious, you will have authority over all evil. Those who walk uprightly I bless! (Read John 15:7.)

April 29

◇

Love and Restoration

**If we confess our sins, He is faithful and just to
forgive us our sins and to cleanse us from
all unrighteousness (1 John 1:9).**

◆

*O Bright and Morning Star, guide me into all
truth. Turn my negatives into positives, my programmed setbacks into fulfillment and creativity.*

I love you . . . unconditionally. I have
known all about you since you were in the
womb. I know how you can reach your highest
potential. I accept you just as you are. Yet I am
changing you into that person you were meant
to be . . . loving, giving, released in your personality . . . all your walls rebuilt and secure. Everything that concerns you concerns Me, and I can
do something about it. My forgiveness is total,
unlike humans who forgive but cannot forget.
Stop feeling guilty. I assure you, your sin is no
longer. It is dead on the cross. Buried, never to
be resurrected. Rejoice in that fact! My love is
making you whole. (Read Romans 8:38–39.)

Worry and Impatience

**Also it is not good for a soul to be without
knowledge, and he sins who hastens
with his feet (Proverbs 19:2).**

♦

*Lord, forgive me for rushing and being annoyed,
for the irritation I feel at the slow pace of others, and
for being dissatisfied today with my own accomplish-
ments. Forgive me for feeling unfulfilled.*

That is a typical symptom of pride and in-
gratitude. You are missing so much when you
hasten, especially the divine radiance that rests
upon those who are grateful. Worry and impatience walk hand-in-hand with busyness, separating you from Me. Do not be deceived . . . all
the effects are negative! All that you are and all
that you will ever be depends upon whether you
abide in Me. Remember that Satan is a *restless*
seeker of whom he may devour. And he will ex-
pend much effort to keep you from being united
with Me, for he knows the power of that bond.
Let My power become your power! (Read John
15:5–7.)

May

Whatever I tell you in the
dark, speak in the light; and
what you hear in the ear,
preach on the housetops.

Matthew 10:27

Awareness

**Let your conduct be without covetousness; be
content with such things as you have. For He
Himself has said, "I will never leave you
nor forsake you" (Hebrews 13:5).**

◆

*Holy Father, thank You for who You are, and for
who I am when I am with You.*

I am with you always, all the way to the end
of the earth. See Me in everything, in the rustle
of the desert palm fronds, the blossom of the
oleander, the budlike flower of the creosote
bush, the purple that changes to indigo after the
spring rains, in the clatter of the roadrunner's
beak and his sobbing moan, the chit-chat chirp-
ings, and the whistlings of the early-morning
bird crowd. See Me in all things. Be aware of the
excitement I have created by My Word. I love
you. And I will never leave you. You can believe
that forever. (Read Psalm 19:1.)

Death to Self

**For this is the will of God, your sanctification;
that you should abstain from sexual immorality;
that each of you should know how to possess
his own vessel in sanctification and honor
(1 Thessalonians 4:3–4).**

◆

Lord, I know "holiness" is for me. And it only comes through the crisis of death and burial of my selfish nature. But . . . I am afraid. I fear if I covenant I cannot be totally pure and uncompromising in my thoughts, unbridled in my devotion. . . .

O child, stop detouring the cemetery and refusing to die. Fear is not of Me! You have come to those "last days" of self many times in word but you have not put it into action. When you truly want My will above all else, you will embrace it as easily and naturally as you walk through the doorway to your kitchen. Delay not the time, for you will look back on this day as a remarkably strengthening experience. Only you can decide. Pray more to know and trust My will! (Read Leviticus 20:7–8.)

May 3

◇

At Rest and Alert

**So he answered and said to me: "This is the word
of the LORD to Zerubbabel: 'Not by might
nor by power, but by My Spirit,' says
the LORD of hosts" (Zechariah 4:6).**

◆

*My Lord, why is it so hard for me to get from
one plateau to the next?*

As you *rest* in My presence I will change you.
Not by might, nor by power are you changed
into My likeness, but by My Spirit. Be released
from the pressure of having to be "spiritual".
Use the mind of Christ that is in you, and *rest*
in Me. Be alert to My Holy Spirit. I love you.
(Read 2 Corinthians 3:17–18.)

Ever-Increasing Love

There is no fear in love; but perfect love casts out fear, because fear involves torment. But he who fears has not been made perfect in love (1 John 4:18).

◆

Lord, help me not to try to impress You with my love. Let it be spontaneous and natural in every way.

Perfection of love is hindered by fear. Be not anxious! The more real I become, the more natural and spontaneous will be the love you feel for Me. Though deep love for Me seems to tarry, child, wait for it—and be surprised when it comes. You are reaching out for more than you have grasped. But I will always inspire you beyond what you can experience. Ever-increasing, everlasting love. (Read Jeremiah 31:3.)

Freedom from Fear

And He said to me, "My grace is sufficient for you, for My strength is made perfect in weakness." Therefore most gladly I will rather boast in my infirmities, that the power of Christ may rest upon me (2 Corinthians 12:9).

◆

Lord, I find myself growing apprehensive about the coming event. Free me from the fear of people's faces and the wasteful wondering of my effect on them.

I will never command you to go where I have not first enabled you. If you use your inability as a barrier to obedience, you have accused Me of shoddy work. Know instead that your lack and dependence open the door of opportunity for My Spirit to manifest power. Do not calculate and estimate, but allow Me to enter in a way that may surprise you. All of a sudden, I will break out on the right hand and on the left. Let this knowledge make your life amazingly simple. Be anxious for nothing. (Read Philippians 4:6–7.)

Fear

**For God has not given us a spirit of fear, but
of power and of love and of a sound
mind (2 Timothy 1:7).**

◆

*Lord, I reaffirm that You have broken through
the wall of fear . . . and now I ask You to demolish
the remnants.*

Whatever you fear is your god. Fear causes
sickness, suspicion, hate, powerlessness, loss of
control, impatience, and an unsound mind.
Fear of man is a snare and stems from pride, the
need to control and to be recognized. It ends in
confusion and shame. But a supernatural fear of
Me, your Father, brings honor, wisdom, faith,
power, health, love, sound-mindedness, power
over body and emotions, supernatural peace,
and freedom. Whatever you fear has power over
you. (Read Galatians 5:1 and Proverbs 29:25.)

Love

**And whatever you do, do it heartily, as to the
Lord and not to men (Colossians 3:23).**

◆

*Make me comfortable to bless those You send for
help, Lord. Only You have words of life.*

I am making you comfortable with all people, peasants and kings. As you humble yourself
and become transparent, everyone will be comfortable in your presence. Love them. It is appropriate for every occasion. Love knocks down
walls and barricades and facades, and unmasks
and unveils others. Love disarms. Love con-
quers. Pray more for love . . . the kind that casts
out fear. Perfect love comes straight from My
throne. Agape (divine) love is never uncomfortable. Nor defeated. Nor unwise. Nor unwilling.
Love always wants My way. (Read Colossians
3:14.)

Poise

**Likewise the Spirit also helps in our weaknesses.
For we do not know what we should pray for
as we ought, but the Spirit Himself makes
intercession for us with groanings which
cannot be uttered (Romans 8:26).**

♦

*Lord, I thank You that how we "feel" when we
pray does not influence the power of our intercession.*

It is a good lesson to learn, that My power
is not dependent upon how you feel. Much
work of My kingdom has been thwarted because of people's dependency upon feelings instead of My Word and My promises. I prefer
that you *know* Me. Develop the mental poise
that comes from being firmly rooted in the eternal truth that I, Your God, am love, am holy,
and hold all durable riches, honor, and righteousness. It is a heroic and courageous thing to
throw yourself upon Me. Do not flinch or waver. You will be surprised by feeling when you
see My marvelous hand at work. (Read Romans
8:27; 1 Timothy 2:1–2 and Proverbs 8:17–18.)

Sickness

**"What do you want Me to do for you?" He
said, "Lord, that I may receive my
sight" (Luke 18:41).**

◆

*Lord, I know it is Your will . . . heal me . . .
and help me receive.*

It does not glorify Me when My children are
sick and sorrowful and defeated. What triumph
is there for Me in that? What glory? Except for
My healthy, joyful, victorious ones who exhibit
My power, how will the world see and want
what sets you apart? Know Me. Trust Me. Feel
Me. Love Me. Bless Me. Obey Me. Rest in Me.
Abide in Me. Believe in Me. And you shall conquer. You shall be triumphant over evil. And
you will glorify Me. That is not to say there will
be no sickness, sorrow, and defeat. But know
that I am the overcomer, and be glad. (Read
1 John 5:4.)

Discipline

For God did not call us to uncleanness, but in holiness (1 Thessalonians 4:7).

◆

Dear Lord, You have called us to be holy as You are holy. How magnificent. How impossible. How?

You cannot save yourself, My child, neither can you sanctify yourself. I do these things. But I will not do what I tell *you* to do! Cultivate good habits; build good character; discipline your footsteps in righteous paths. Control yourself. Be patient and sincere. I give you power over all the power of Satan. Use it! And never say no to Me. Let praise or blame be all the same. Abandon yourself to My love and power, and the impression left will be that of My holiness, never of your own person. I will prove to be more than you ever dreamed I would be. (Read Luke 10:19.)

◇

Holiness

Husbands, love your wives, just as Christ also loved the church and gave Himself for her, that He might sanctify and cleanse her with the washing of water by the word, that He might present her to Himself a glorious church, not having spot or wrinkle or any such thing, but that she should be holy and without blemish (Ephesians 5:25–27).

♦

Lord, why is there such prejudice among believers?

Because My own will not listen to what they hear. Because of unbelief. I call My own to be a holy people . . . whole and lacking nothing. I am coming back for a church without a spot or wrinkle, a church that has learned to love. Do not be the cause for delay. Be ready. Have nothing in your hands that is not easy for you to lay down. Grasp after nothing. Release all to Me. Hold onto no person, place, or thing that would act as a magnet holding you to earth. (Read Deuteronomy 14:2.)

Inexhaustible Strength

Have you not known? Have you not heard? The everlasting God, the LORD, the Creator of the ends of the earth, neither faints nor is weary. His understanding is unsearchable
(Isaiah 40:28).

◆

It was an impossible week when I looked at it from the other side. Thank You, Lord, for keeping me supplied with "fresh springs."

Are you surprised that I am the everlasting God, the Lord, the Creator who faints not, nor grows weary? I give power to those who have no might, and increase strength! You would be drained to the dregs and utterly exhausted if you had not relied on Me for your supply. Always seek your power source—the foundation of your love, peace, and compassion—where you will find a constant and plenteous flow. You are mortal! I am inexhaustible! Wait upon Me, and renew your strength! (Read Isaiah 40:29–31.)

May 13

◇

Concentration

You will keep him in perfect peace, whose mind is stayed on You, because he trusts in You (Isaiah 26:3).

◆

You asked Your disciples to "watch" with You and they fell asleep. Isn't it just as negligent when I wander away in my thoughts, pondering the day and its duties? Lord, let my greatest duty be that of practicing Your presence. Teach me the power of concentration and how to use my imagination creatively.

Picture concentration as the helmet of salvation. Protected and safe inside is imagination, created by Me. From every direction come imaginings. Put up the shield of faith. Practice believing. Pursue the Father. Your imagination will be creative, sharp, and active as long as you use it for good. The test of whether your concentration is given to Me is how easily you bring the imagination into captivity. Rouse yourself. Refuse to allow your mind to be "used." Deliberately reject Satan's suggestions and turn to Me, your ever-present help. (Read Romans 8:5.)

Introspection

But avoid foolish and ignorant disputes, knowing that they generate strife. And a servant of the Lord must not quarrel but be gentle to all, able to teach, patient (2 Timothy 2:23–24).

◆

Lord, make me an instrument of Your peace . . . for Your glory.

Beloved, your spiritual life need not be continually before your eyes, as were the sins of David, for I never intended you to be a museum. If you endlessly investigate and internalize, you have become overly conscious of becoming virtuous, or patient, godly, or peaceful—or lacking in those qualities. When every virtue is so automatic as to be a habit, you will have no consciousness of it, nor the constant need to seek it. Then comes divine peace. Stop striving to be at a certain place. Simply live the life of Jesus—who was at all times and every place comfortable, humble, and simply Himself. (Read Ephesians 4:1–3.)

May 15

◇

Hearing God

For he who has entered His rest has himself also
ceased from his works as God did from His. Let
us therefore be diligent to enter that rest, lest
anyone fall according to the same example
of disobedience (Hebrews 4:10–11).

♦

*Lord, show me how to enter into the rest that I
seem so short of, the rest of faith which listens and
believes utterly.*

Perfect hearing comes from a deeper identifi-
cation of your spirit with My Son, Jesus. What
hinders is involvement with other things (even
good things). Let not the loud drum drown out
the sweetness of My melody. I speak! And if you
delight in obeying, I will instantly press to the
front of your life. Stay fit! Do not give in to self-
pity or grumbling or disagreeableness. Not to
the rushed and pressed do I come, but to the fit
and resting. Labor to enter into that rest. (Read
Mark 11:22.)

Rest

**So we see that they could not enter in
because of unbelief (Hebrews 3:19).**

◆

*Lord, I feel so dense, but I cannot seem to climb
over that barrier between You and me. Tell me again
about rest.*

You are not dense, but you have not obeyed
Me enthusiastically, either. I say, "arise and
walk," "stretch forth your hand," and yours is
the next move. Rest is a simple word. Why do
you complicate it? Some cannot enter into rest
because of unbelief . . . some because of will-
fulness. I created and rested. My people must
rest. (Read Jeremiah 6:16.)

Divine Guidance

**Then as he lay and slept under a broom tree,
suddenly an angel touched him, and said to
him, "Arise and eat" (1 Kings 19:5).**

◆

O Lord, let Your Word be life to me today.

Arise and eat.

But, Lord, You know I am fasting.

Arise and eat. I am the One who calls you
to fast and I am the One who ends it.

*Yes, Lord. But how can I be sure this is not my
flesh wanting to eat?*

The power that made you restless has been
put to flight. So, arise, obey, and eat!

*Hallelujah! You are a great God! Your way and
Your timing is marvelous.* (Read Isaiah 58:6 and
Colossians 3:15.)

Preparation

**The Lord GOD has given Me the tongue of the
learned, that I should know how to speak a
word in season to him who is weary. He awakens
Me morning by morning, He awakens My
ear to hear as the learned (Isaiah 50:4).**

◆

*Lord, I do not want to walk in the light of my
own fire, or be encompassed about with my own
sparks; I want the fire of Your Holy Spirit.*

I have given you a tongue to speak, to one or
to multitudes. And I awaken all of your abilities
morning by morning. Be not afraid, for I give
you power to deliver. I, who dry up the seas
with one word and make rivers in the desert,
would I make you ashamed for waiting upon
Me? In your dream you were ill-prepared to ad-
dress a group. I alert you to *be ready* in season
and out of season . . . as a healthy tomato plant
bearing rich, ripe tomatoes stands tall in the
winter snow. I am preparing you now to stand,
to listen, to hear My voice, to speak with authority and wisdom. (Read 2 Timothy 4:2.)

Despair

**Rise, let us be going. See, My betrayer
is at hand (Mark 14:42).**

♦

*Lord, keep us from despair . . . the kind that
comes when we realize that we have missed a wonderful opportunity; that tells us it is "too late"; that
provokes misery, regret over unwise counsel or a misplaced investment.*

When My disciples slept that night in Geth-
semane, then fled and denied Me, they felt utter
despair—as if that opportunity was lost forever.
And it was! But now as then, I say: "Rise up,
let us go." Never allow the cloak of failure to
cling to you. Shake it off and move forward under My certain leadership. Trust utterly in Me.
I will restore everything the cankerworm has
eaten. Only look back to learn, then on to the
next thing, where you will be more than conquerors. Not by your own ingenuity shall it be
so, but by the fact that My love is constant toward you. And love is unconquerable. (Read
Romans 8:37.)

Power and Authority

And I will give you the keys of the kingdom of heaven, and whatever you bind on earth will be bound in heaven, and whatever you loose on earth will be loosed in heaven (Matthew 16:19).

◆

Your power is awesome, Lord, how great Thou art!

Yes. And I have given you My power and authority on earth: whatever you bind on earth shall be bound in heaven, and whatever you loose on earth shall be loosed in heaven. With this kind of authority, you have the grave responsibility to take care what you speak, what you pray, what you seek, and what your example says. I expect much from those who call Me Lord . . . but it is little when seen in the light of what you receive. (Read Zechariah 8:16–17.)

May 21

◇

Genuine Prayer

Watch and pray, lest you enter into temptation. The spirit indeed is willing, but the flesh is weak (Matthew 26:41).

◆

It is an honor to "watch," Lord. Keep me alert I pray.

I have fully equipped you to watch! Alertness with perseverance means a disciplined and vigilant sentinel, ever watchful for approaching enemies, ready for spiritual conflict. Genuine prayer disallows a dull, drowsy state, dawdling phrases, or mindless words. Do not allow your mind to wander or skip, become indifferent or ritualistic. Think when you pray! Remember that you are speaking to your majestic Father. (Read Ephesians 6:18.)

From Glory to Glory

**By your patience possess your souls
(Luke 21:19).**

◆

Lord, I have need of patience!

Be still, and know that I am God. As you get nearer and nearer, you will take on more and more of My characteristics. You will identify them as My characteristics because they are so different from yours. You will become more like Me and more like your true self—changed from glory to glory, from sinful to sinless, from grasping to giving, from needing to serving, from anxious pressing to peaceful orderliness, from seeking your own way to a glad acceptance of change. Once you really see Me as I Am, the most impossible things will be done as easily as breathing. But there is a veil between us that needs to come down. It is so thin you hardly notice it is there. But you will know when you have cast it aside for then you will see clearly, and patience will have her perfect work! Courage! Courage! (Read 1 John 3:2.)

◇

Faith

"What do you want Me to do for you?" He said, "Lord, that I may receive my sight." Then Jesus said to him, "Receive your sight; your faith has made you well" (Luke 18:41–42).

◆

Lord, You've said the "yoke shall be destroyed because of the anointing," but the veil between us only I can remove. I do not know what the veil is, Father, but I believe it's there because You said so. Give me vision to see it.

By faith, Noah prepared. By faith, Abraham obeyed. Through faith, Sarah received. And through belief and humility, Moses executed My commands. Faith allows one to pass through the Red Sea. Faith brings the walls down. Faith has won kingdoms, obtained promises, closed lions' mouths, quenched fire, made the weak strong and the dead rise. When you hear, "receive your sight," that is the time to take off the veil and rip it to shreds. By faith, "receive your sight." Do it! (Read Luke 18:43; Isaiah 58:9–11 and Hebrews 11:1.)

Fascinating Prospects

Knowing this, that our old man was crucified with Him, that the body of sin might be done away with, that we should no longer be slaves of sin (Romans 6:6).

◆

Lord, the hardest thing for me to believe is that I could be so identified with You that there is nothing of the old "me" left.

My Son, Jesus, is the enabling power and agency through which you live. Just as air is all around as well as in you, it is the same principle for living in Christ. I have made you a new creature; the old passed away. You are established in Christ, through whom you walk and have your being—bold and wise and whole. Never give up because a thing seems beyond you, but allow His inner surge of power to energize your body, mind, and spirit. And one day, because you believe and allow Me to have My way, you will awake and find that your old nature is truly transformed. (Read Ephesians 1:8 and Philemon 6.)

May 25

◇

Fear

There is no fear in love; but perfect love casts out fear, because fear involves torment. But he who fears has not been made perfect in love (1 John 4:18).

♦

O Lord, this situation is so painful. . . .

Let not your spirit fidget nor your soul fear. Strike anxiety and fear with mighty blows, as you might a thief entering your home through a window. These can steal much more than material goods; their target is your peace and joy. Don't just give a glancing blow or one only meant to stun. Aim to kill! Drive a stake into the heart of fear, anxiety, oppression, and pride. Let love stand over them triumphant, as the satisfaction of the Lord washes over you in great billows. (Read Ephesians 6:10–13.)

Self-Addiction

**And whoever exalts himself will be humbled,
and he who humbles himself will be
exalted (Matthew 23:12).**

◆

*I thank You, Lord, for the opportunity to over-
come. Even as I ask for the strength to humble myself,
I am seeking respect and recognition. What a war!*

When it is over, dear one, you will be left
standing triumphant and more qualified to use
My authority with power. You will be strengthened by *giving* and *giving up*. Jesus sacrificed
Himself, and I sacrificed My only Son, that you
might be free of this self-addiction. Let Me convert this strong drive, this passionate yearning to
be somebody, into energy which will make you
a transparent somebody through whom the
light and life of Jesus can be seen—somebody
that makes others see and want what you have.
(Read Luke 14:11.)

Grace

**And if by grace, then it is no longer of works;
otherwise grace is no longer grace
(Romans 11:6).**

◆

*Lord, give me grace to discipline my tongue . . .
grace not to be easily shaken.*

This is an eternal law: as you die to self, your discipline and diligence in the physical will be manifest in the spiritual. It is already happening! I give My grace unto you, which you have not merited, nor can you understand, for the marvel of My love exhibited on the cross is unfathomable. Receive the quickening life of My Holy Spirit, and let your face be undaunted, radiant all the time because of My unalterable love. Let go and lay hold of Me, that I may make you fit for all that I require of you. My grace is sufficient for you. (Read Hebrews 12:28 and 2 Corinthians 12:9.)

Relinquishment

**Now the Lord is the Spirit; and where the
Spirit of the Lord is, there is liberty
(2 Corinthians 3:17).**

◆

*Lord, give me perfect liberty. Let that liberation
be so real in me that the message will liberate others.
I will gather the material but You must set it aflame.*

Where My Holy Spirit is, there is liberty.
You have persevered, waiting for a vision that
tarried. You have passed the test of loyalty.
Now, you will live in the light of what you have
seen. I am ready to send you out, but do not
go ahead of Me. Your choice would prove
empty, while Mine will produce good fruit.
Abandon yourself to Me—not to be free of sin,
or to be made holy, or to be delivered, or
taught—but out of love for Me. Do not calculate or weigh the cost, for true relinquishment
is never conscious of itself or rewards, only of
the magnificent One to whom all is surrendered. (Read Hebrews 13:8.)

Live Today

In that day you will ask in My name, and I do
not say to you that I shall pray the Father for
you; for the Father Himself loves you, because
you have loved Me, and have believed that I
came forth from God (John 16:26–27).

◆

*Lord, put us where You want us this day, within
Your reach.*

A submitted attitude is infinitely valuable.
As My followers make ready to be used, they are
headed for high purposes . . . My purposes . . .
always higher than anything you have planned
for yourself. I have only promised you strength
for each day, so take care not to waste time on
sins and failures of yesterday, nor on fears for tomorrow, for "you have not gained godly wisdom to bear the burdens of the Holy One." No
regrets. No fears. Just an instrument clean and
ready for today . . . an extension of My hand.
"In that day, you will ask in My name" *is* today,
here and now. A day for Me to reveal to you My
counsel, My wisdom. (Read Proverbs 30:3.)

A Yielded Attitude

Do you not know that to whom you present yourselves slaves to obey, you are that one's slaves whom you obey, whether of sin leading to death, or of obedience leading to righteousness? (Romans 6:16).

◆

Lord, I submit to You . . . no fears . . . no regrets.

It is good that you are yielded to Me, for whatever you bow to—person or habit—will dominate. Yielding to Jesus breaks all the chains and sets you free to learn to live in My light. Drag any soulish moods or carnal criticisms in front of My heavenly searchlight, for if you try to hide from Me you will become withdrawn and hard. The penalty of sin is that you gradually become accustomed to it and forget that it is sin. Do not argue or look to others for excuses or confirmation of your morality, but let your inner watchfulness yield continually to My Spirit. Your reward is unspeakable joy. (Read 2 Corinthians 7:1.)

May 31

◇

Transformed by Obedience

**So Jesus answered and said to them,
"Have faith in God" (Mark 11:22).**

◆

*Lord, restore and revitalize those things which
were stunted in us when we were but children. Cause
us yet to be all that You envisioned. . . .*

My ultimate purpose is that My Son be
formed in you, your life transformed by obedience to Him . . . down to the last thing that has
been stunted in your personality. All is redeemed! Then you become responsible for
keeping your spirit in agreement with My Holy
Spirit—putting Me first, trusting Me wholly.
Faith never knows where it is being led, only
that it is. Finally you come to know the reason
you can mount up with wings as eagles is because of a life of walking and not fainting, of being tried and proven. This is the secret the world
does not know: Intimacy with Me is the key to
everything of worth. Delight yourself in Me.
And I will give you the desires of your heart.
(Read Hebrews 11:6.)

June

And with many such parables
He spoke the word to them as
they were able to hear it.

Mark 4:33

June 1

◇

That I May Increase

Blessed are the pure in heart, for they shall see God (Matthew 5:8).

◆

Lord, help me to stop defending myself and to walk in the light, confessing easily and instantly, baring myself before You when I am wrong. And when right, give me the grace to answer as Jesus did, with not a word. Help me be a peacemaker!

Holiness is not of a proper order if it is not humble and does not draw to Me. If you increase in the eyes of men, instead of decrease so they can see Jesus, your influence has been misdirected. Make sure your desire for sanctity or service does not become the means whereby your soul avoids Me. It is a subtle deception! If your vision at any point becomes less than clear, stop everything until you get things in proper perspective again. Vision always depends on integrity of character. The pure in heart *see* Me. (Read John 3:30 and 2 Corinthians 3:3.)

Transformed

A new commandment I give to you, that you love one another; as I have loved you, that you also love one another (John 13:34).

♦

Dear precious Lord, thank You for our marriage and Your peace.

Happy anniversary, dear ones. You have been transformed from a defensive, contending, competitive couple to one not easily offended or confounded. Your minds and emotions are being purified by obeying the truth, so that you truly love one another with pure hearts. By your sacrifice of self you honor one another, and become more like My Son, who has no guile. Continue to grow in faith and good conscience toward each other, for your lives speak as My oracles, the oracles of Almighty God. (Read John 15:12.)

June 3

◇

Failure

Then He answered and spoke to those who
stood before Him, saying, "Take away the filthy
garments from him." And to him He said,
"See, I have removed your iniquity from
you, and I will clothe you with
rich robes" (Zechariah 3:4).

◆

O Lord, when will I stop failing You?

Behold, I have caused your iniquity to pass
from you and I hold out to you a new change
of clothing. There will come a time. . . . (Read
Isaiah 53:6.)

Healing

There He made a statute and an ordinance for
them, and there He tested them, and said,
"If you diligently heed the voice of the LORD
your God and do what is right in His sight,
give ear to His commandments and keep all His
statutes, I will put none of the diseases on
you which I have brought on the Egyptians.
For I am the LORD who heals you"
(Exodus 15:25–26).

◆

*Dear Jesus, intercede for me. My body needs Your
gracious touch.*

I know you by name, and I will do this thing
you have asked, and I will give you rest. If you
will diligently hearken to My voice, do what is
right, give ear to My commands, and keep all
My statutes, you will have none of these diseases
on you, for I am the Lord who heals and keeps
you! (Read Matthew 4:24.)

Rest

**Have mercy upon me, O God, according to
Your lovingkindness; according to the
multitude of Your tender mercies, blot
out my transgressions (Psalm 51:1).**

◆

Lord, I feel so inadequate for the task ahead.

Bow your head and I will bless you. Anxious
thoughts and tired nerves be gone! Receive My
lovingkindness, My tenderness. Rest. I will take
care of you. (Read Hebrews 4:11.)

Guard Your Thoughts

For to be carnally minded is death, but to be spiritually minded is life and peace (Romans 8:6).

◆

Renew my mind, dear Father, I feel so sluggish and spent.

Stop all imaginings! Keep a watch over yourself, for Satan's first attempt at treachery is directed toward the mind and emotions. Stand alert! Do not allow your mind to be used as a dumping station or a negative reactor. Act! Be first in good thoughts, good reactions. Never let your mind dwell on anything evil, lustful, sickly, critical, hateful, or fearful. Keep yourself in an attitude of mental and emotional praise, peaceful and loving, constantly pulling your thoughts back into channels of heavenly resource. Be aware of My angels surrounding you. (Read Ephesians 4:23.)

June 7

◇

Beauty of Holiness

**Of the increase of His government and peace
there will be no end, upon the throne of David
and over His kingdom, to order it and establish
it with judgment and justice from that time
forward, even forever (Isaiah 9:7).**

◆

Deliver me from pointless thinking, O God.

I have blessed you with all you need to
change your nature. And as you change, you
grow, are growing even now, in grace and power
and beauty, the beauty of holiness. The mind of
Christ is in you. My Holy Spirit courses
through you. My great, unchangeable creativity
with which I created the universe surrounds
you. I am teaching you to focus on Me and stay
concentrated for longer and longer periods. Do
not concern yourself, just remain available, and
My zeal will perform it. (Read Ephesians 2:8–
11.)

Rejoice in Discipline

**But we have this treasure in earthen vessels,
that the excellence of the power may be of
God and not of us (2 Corinthians 4:7).**

◆

I believe in You, Lord.

I believe in you, My child.

I trust You, Lord.

I trust you, child.

I need You, dear wonderful Jesus.

I need you also. I can only work in the world
through the brave, true, and strong who listen
and obey. Rejoice as I discipline and train you,
so that My power working through you may
quickly win the world. When you choose the
way that prospers the soul, a wonderful shaping
occurs—allowing prayers to be answered, troubles and grief to be dispelled, and many to receive you and Me. (Read 2 Corinthians 4:8–10.)

June 9

◇

Confidence

**But we all, with unveiled face, beholding as in
a mirror the glory of the Lord, are being
transformed into the same image from
glory to glory, just as by the Spirit of
the Lord (2 Corinthians 3:18).**

◆

*Lord, change me! How can You stand me the way
I am?*

I love you. And you are being changed by
My Spirit. Keep your eyes ever on Me, but be
alert to your very real enemy, Satan, who attempts to stop your progress at every point. Do
not worry. Although he may be able to overwhelm *you,* I am greater. As you are Mine, all of
My power becomes yours for all I command you
to do. Learn how to appropriate it at a moment's notice—emptied of self and doubt, depending on Me alone, trusting My right
direction, clinging to Me. Confident! (Read
1 John 4:4 and Philippians 1:6.)

Fear and Affliction

The LORD has appeared of old to me, saying:
"Yes, I have loved you with an everlasting
love; therefore with lovingkindness I
have drawn you" (Jeremiah 31:3).

◆

*Lord, I confess I've reserved a part of myself that
is afraid of You. I have prayed for perfection as You
are perfect, and holiness as You are holy, but with the
suspicion that the answer might contain suffering or
sorrow with it . . . just as the great grapevines of
France must suffer and struggle up through the worst
kind of soil to give the world the finest wines. I confess
my reservation and lack of trust, and hereby repent
and abandon myself to You.*

My child, do not seek affliction, and do not
fear it, for I am with you in all. I love you more
than you could ever love yourself. (Read Proverbs 10:22.)

June 11

◇

Come unto Me

Come to Me, all you who labor and are heavy laden, and I will give you rest (Matthew 11:28).

♦

Lord, strengthen me for the chaotic week before me.

Come unto Me for majestic vitality. Come unto Me and let go of all else. Come unto Me to be freed from weariness and exhaustion in your body, mind, and spirit. Come unto Me to be cleansed. Come unto Me to be healed. Come unto Me to be made whole. Come unto Me for *peace* and *rest*. Come unto Me for creativity—and life itself. (Read Ephesians 2:14.)

◇

Good Character

Therefore, my beloved brethren, be steadfast, immovable, always abounding in the work of the Lord, knowing that your labor is not in vain in the Lord (1 Corinthians 15:58).

♦

Lord, thank You for the beauty of friends, fellowship, and wise counsel.

It is truly I who draw people to you. But it is steadfast, immovable character which holds their attention. Good character is not something one is born with, or reborn with; it is something acquired as you trust in Me . . . as you call Me Lord, and do the things I say. Daily . . . moment to moment . . . listen for My guidance. Wait for My next touch of power. Rest in My peace. Experience My love in all. Extend it to all. (Read Romans 5:1–5.)

June 13

◇

Power and Authority

Behold, I give you the authority to trample
on serpents and scorpions, and over all the
power of the enemy, and nothing shall
by any means hurt you (Luke 10:19).

◆

*Lord, we are being surrounded and engulfed.
Help us!*

Do not pray for Me to get rid of Satan for
you! I have given you that power and authority.
Rather, pray for spiritual eyes to see into the
darkness, for your understanding to be enlight-
ened, for a lifting of the veil that you may see
into the dark corners and recognize the enemy
there. See him camouflaged against that back-
ground where he blends in so well you can
scarcely make out a form. Pray for the subtleties
of your adversary to become clear to you. Pray
for a skillful and extraordinary talent with which
to use the tools I have given you. (Read Ephesians 6:10–11.)

Rest in Me

If you abide in Me, and My words abide in you, you will ask what you desire, and it shall be done for you (John 15:7).

◆

Show us how to abide in You, O Lord, whether we are working, shopping, entertaining, speaking, writing, studying, or resting in the desert.

Wherever your body is, be "at home." If you wait until this trial is over, this job finished, or this week past to start abiding, then you need to work on impudence and self-consideration. My command to you today is "rest in Me, abide in Me." You cannot bear fruit in and of yourself. But if you abide in Me and My words abide in you, you shall ask what you will, and it shall be done unto you. Then My desire will be your will. And what you produce will glorify Me. I bless you to "abide in Me." Whoever abides does not sin! (Read 1 John 3:6.)

June 15

◇

Shaped and Sharpened

**Therefore do not be ashamed of the testimony
of our Lord, nor of me His prisoner, but share
with me in the sufferings for the gospel
according to the power of God, who has saved
us and called us with a holy calling, not
according to our works, but according to His
own purpose and grace which was given to us
in Christ Jesus before time began
(2 Timothy 1:8–9).**

◆

Lord, here I am. Use me!

Yes. You are My instrument. You have been
tempered and shaped to fit the specific tasks you
were meant to do. I have sharpened your personality to cut through the superfluous, and
whittled you to fit perfectly into My design. You
are now being polished to make you graceful,
poised, and usable. Each of my instruments
must wait for the thrill of My touch, My timing, My song. Learn to wait and watch and be
ready. (Read Romans 8:28–29.)

Guard Your Tongue

Keep your tongue from evil, and your lips from speaking deceit. Depart from evil and do good; seek peace and pursue it (Psalm 34:13–14).

◆

I renounce any hidden thing of dishonesty, O God, and I commend myself to Your conscience. Help me to think before I speak.

Take care not to speak foolishly or entertain doubt and disbelief, for you may get what you speak. A wise person restrains the tongue. Guard your tongue! Be bold to honor My directives, persevering and single-minded as an athlete. (Read Proverbs 21:13 and 29:11.)

June 17

◇

Changed Character

I love those who love me, and those who seek me diligently will find me (Proverbs 8:17).

◆

Show me how to make more room in me for You, Lord.

Cease all struggle. Open your hands. Let your shoulders relax. Free yourself of all concerns. If you will eagerly seek for Me, not waiting for a great disaster before you learn to rest in Me, then you will be prepared when difficulties arise. And if you will "abide" in Me, most problems will never arise. Remember to seek Me early. Before confusion, problems, excitement, or even good works crowd Me out. These times with Me are times of greater significance than you can realize now. Even so, take care not to worship the habit of meeting Me. Worship *Me!* It is not the habit that makes this holy hour holy, but the quality of your love and obedience that counts. Thereby is your character changed. (Read Psalm 95:6–7.)

Abide in Me

Nevertheless I have this against you, that you have left your first love (Revelation 2:4).

♦

Lord, help me to turn to You first when I have a problem . . . my first love!

Minds and tongues that worship Me but not in spirit, will look away from Me in times of trouble also. When eyes are turned from Me to another, to one's self, or to a circumstance, they are not seeing spiritually. When you are ready, you never have to get ready. If you are resting and abiding in Me, when I call or when you need Me, there will be no wasted time. I will be "living in" all the time. The burning bush is always ablaze with My presence, amazingly present and burning, yet never consumed. (Read Psalm 91:1.)

June 19

◇

Obedience

Is this not the fast that I have chosen: to loose
the bonds of wickedness, to undo the heavy
burdens, to let the oppressed go free, and that
you break every yoke? Is it not to share your
bread with the hungry, and that you bring to
your house the poor who are cast out; when
you see the naked, that you cover him, and
not hide yourself from your own flesh?
(Isaiah 58:6–7).

◆

Let this fast be acceptable in Your sight, O Lord.

You have followed the path of obedience
which leads to My throne. This fast is a fast of
release—to undo you from a heavy burden.
Watch for your light to break forth as the morning and your health to spring forth speedily.
Rely not on a past relationship with Me but
allow Me to do a new thing, careful not to com-
pare our relationship with that of others. (Read
Matthew 17:21.)

Thankfulness

And the LORD restored Job's losses when he prayed for his friends. Indeed the LORD gave Job twice as much as he had before (Job 42:10).

◆

Happy Father's Day, Lord! Thank You for being our Abba-Father, our Daddy-God . . . thank You for everything.

You have "everything" because of My Son's atonement. As you abide in Me, all My power is yours as it was His. The real thrust of His life was, and is, intercessory prayer. (Read Romans 5:8–9.)

June 21

◇

Joy in My Presence

I will instruct you and teach you in the way you should go; I will guide you with My eye (Psalm 32:8).

◆

Lord, prepare us for the week to come. Let everything come together easily, with great thankfulness, praise, and love among us all.

I promise you *release*. You shall be shielded from the storm. My joy shall be your strength. My presence will strengthen and instruct you, and you will walk calmly, inspiring peace in others, seeing them as I see them. Do not be morbidly introspective, looking forward with dread anticipation, but stay alert! Be not handicapped by tomorrow. Rest . . . in the midst of celebration. (Read Revelation 3:21.)

Practice My Presence

**Behold, I stand at the door and knock. If
anyone hears My voice and opens the door,
I will come in to him and dine with him,
and he with Me (Revelation 3:20).**

◆

Come in, Lord, and sit with me a while.

I have opened a door that no man can shut,
but you have the screen locked in place. As I
call, you hear My voice in every room and even
see My glory. Now, fiber by fiber, I want you to
remove the net between us . . . that I may come
and dine with you.

What screen, Lord?

You look at Me as at a painting whose grainy
canvas still seeps into the awareness; I would have
you see Me with absolute clarity, that you may
cling to Me in the hour of temptation.

I want to see Your refined image, Lord.

Then do not keep Me at a distance. (Read
Hebrews 10:22.)

June 23

◇

Wasteful Thinking

**Keep your heart with all diligence, for out of it
spring the issues of life (Proverbs 4:23).**

◆

*Holy Spirit, admonish me whenever I begin to lose
myself in my own thoughts, wishes, people, or things
that keep me from following conversation with You or
others. Open my eyes to the real reality. . . . Jesus,
and Your absolute Holiness.*

And your own iniquities. Let there be
no more fleeing into a make-believe or pointless thought life, absentmindedness or idle-
mindedness which separates Me from you. You
have the light and discriminating keenness,
courage, and spiritual backbone to make a thor-
ough break with unreality *now*. Be diligent in
this effort so that your days and activity will
yield immortal fruit. (Read Proverbs 4:25, 26.)

Rest—a Joint Venture

For thus says the Lord GOD, the Holy One of
Israel: "In returning and rest you shall be
saved; in quietness and confidence shall be your
strength." But you would not (Isaiah 30:15).

◆

*O power of God, be our stamina this day—let
Your virtue flow over and through my body. . . .*

I speak *rest* to you. Sit by the well and rest.
Allow all of your body to sink into Me, every
muscle relaxed, every thought of health and My
capacity to heal and deliver. Feel Me. Touch the
hem of His garment who sits at My right hand,
interceding for you this moment. Beware of any
work that enables you to evade Me. Concentrate on Me! And all the margins of your life will
fall into order. If you concentrate on the work
instead of Me, it weighs heavy on your neck and
back—pressing down, bending, burdening. But
as you concentrate on Me, I take the burden
and you are free. Hear Me. It is a joint venture.
Believe Me! (Read Proverbs 4:23 and Philippians 2:21.)

June 25

◇

Protection

**Grace and peace be multiplied to you in
the knowledge of God and of Jesus
our Lord (2 Peter 1:2).**

◆

*Lord, help my first response to be to get involved
when I see someone in trouble. Not like those who saw
the rapist with the dagger and did not lift a hand to
help the woman.*

Learn the lesson she learned without the
catalyst she had. As she lifted her eyes from the
struggle, she saw those watching and realized
that her cries for help were to no avail. There is
only One in all the universe who can help. I,
the Almighty, deliver those who call upon Me
out of the hand of the adversary. The lesson is
to have My name on the tip of your tongue. Do
not leave yourself unprotected. In return, when
you see the sorrowful and unsaved and have the
means to save them, do something. Be fearless
to save others. The power is Mine: Love. (Read
2 Peter 1:3.)

Guard Your Tongue

Even so the tongue is a little member and
boasts great things. See how great a forest a
little fire kindles! And the tongue is a fire, a
world of iniquity. The tongue is so set among
our members that it defiles the whole body,
and sets on fire the course of nature; and
it is set on fire by hell (James 3:5–6).

◆

*Lord, cause this aggravating pain in my mouth
to cease, I pray.*

I see the rough spot left on your filling, how
it antagonizes and aggravates the soft tissue of
the tongue as it rubs against it. Learn from the
soreness that has developed, and guard your
tongue so it does not become a vehicle of torment, aggravation, or aggressiveness. Submit
your mouth to Me, the Most High God, so that
I may fill it with wisdom, words of knowledge,
discernment, and encouragement. Be filled up
with My love. (Read 2 Peter 3:11 and Proverbs
21:23.)

◇

Grace

And He said to me, "My grace is sufficient for you, for My strength is made perfect in weakness." Therefore most gladly I will rather boast in my infirmities, that the power of Christ may rest upon me (2 Corinthians 12:9).

◆

Lord, help us to release those people into Your hands who are unlovable or who have grieved us.

Dear one, draw on My grace. Not after lengthy prayer, not after drawing away for a special anointed time. Now! You are not called upon to endure . . . the time is now. When you have a rich account from which to draw, why wait and suffer? My grace is sufficient. Draw now! Then pour out grace. When love is in operation, then grace abounds to chastise or discipline where you are in the position of authority to do so. Or to love the unlovables. Seek Me now—for every situation! And you will be richly endowed to handle it. (Read Zechariah 4:7.)

Cleansing

Judge not, that you be not judged. For with what judgment you judge, you will be judged; and with the measure you use, it will be measured back to you (Matthew 7:1–2).

◆

O my God, give us [all the Body of Christ] beauty for ashes. Cleanse us, O righteous Father, that we may be without spot or wrinkle, for You. Purify us . . . of that which we know and that which is as yet unrecognized.

I have sent a spirit of repentance for My church. Open your hearts to receive. Let My Spirit convict you personally. Allow exposure to the sin of others to reach you personally, to uncover sin in you. Then you will not be burdened by their failure but you will be convicted of sin in self . . . and you will not look with reproach but with sorrow and a penitent heart. Let faith arise to cleanse and purify. Let love arise—to forgive others and yourself. Let hope arise—confident that others will be able to overcome. (Read Matthew 7:1–5 and 2 Peter 3:9, 14.)

June 29

◇

Faith and Forgiveness

Therefore whoever humbles himself as this little child is the greatest in the kingdom of heaven (Matthew 18:4).

◆

Forgive me for small-mindedness, Lord, and for withholding good things in my heart.

Whenever you seek Me with an open and penitent heart you are forgiven. I withhold nothing good from My children. You are forgiven. Now, go forward and forget, except for remembering to be large-minded in your ability to forgive others. Then watch your life become supercharged with surprises, eliminating the death of believing in unbelief or believing in a belief. Believe only in Me! Let Me make you as flexible in your views as a little child, open to receive My unwavering Word, My flawless guidance . . . not attempting to guess what it is, just resting in the comforting knowledge that My way is always right. It is a glorious certainty. (Read Luke 11:28.)

◇

Love

**And we have known and believed the love that
God has for us. God is love, and he who
abides in love abides in God, and
God in him (1 John 4:16).**

◆

*Pour a double portion of love into me, Lord, for
that aggravating person. Help me to see that person
with Your eyes.*

Love is not premeditated. It is spontaneous.
When I build in you My character, it becomes
your first nature. I am love—not in your heart
naturally, but supernaturally. Trying to prove or
defend your love is a sure sign it is lacking. The
sign that you love Me is that you obey Me.
Bring yourself to judgment quickly. If you do
not, an inexorable process begins which makes
life more difficult. I want to spare you. Be good
to yourself. Abide in Me and you shall have all
the love you need, given without forethought.
Love never fails. (Read 1 Corinthians 13:4–8.)

July

**Therefore take heed
how you hear.**

Luke 8:18

◇

Holiness

But as He who called you is holy, you also be holy in all your conduct, because it is written, "Be holy, for I am holy" (1 Peter 1:15–16).

◆

Sometimes I feel so inadequate and ignorant, Lord . . . like this morning.

Be holy as I am holy. I would not ask it if it were not possible. Be whole . . . in every area of your being—body, soul, and spirit. Be free from fear of every sort; and free from self-consideration, with liberty to speak at any moment. Trust Me for all the answers. Speak aloud My written Word and promises. Be vigilant to attack and overthrow thoughts of lack and imaginary situations of failure. Cast them aside as a deadly serpent ready to strike. Think of success in each situation. See My point of view, and know that My power will never fail. Be confident, for yours is to be a double portion. (Read 1 Thessalonians 4:7.)

Childlike Laughter

A merry heart does good, like medicine, but a broken spirit dries the bones (Proverbs 17:22).

♦

Lord, the way seems so stony and laden with briars. What must I do?

Not one stone will trip you nor any briar scratch you, if you listen and follow My guidance. Simply lay down your cares and let childlike laughter rise within you. Face these coming days with a brave and happy heart. Be of good courage, for the enemy is under your feet and you are seated with Me in heavenly places. There is nothing ethereal in this; it is a simple fact. You have much in your life to provoke ready laughter, simple trust, fearlessness, and joy. Today is sublimely sweet. Do not miss it in striving to know or plan for tomorrow. (Read Genesis 21:6.)

July 3

◇

A Servant's Heart

. . . with goodwill doing service, as to the
Lord, and not to men (Ephesians 6:7).

♦

*Death-dealing sorrows encompass me as the ag-
gravations of hell assault us. Give me the heart of a
servant, Lord, when my soul wants to run away. Help
me to act, not react. Make me a channel of Your love.*

A servant's heart seeks nothing for itself, and
does not resent receiving nothing. In exchange
for the moodiness, depression, and criticism of
others, give love . . . being thankful for the opportunity to overcome. As you triumph over
yourself, your enemy, and the circumstances,
you actually defeat Satan's evil pleasure. But you
must keep your eyes off yourself and on Me . . .
to give freely. Open your mouth with wisdom
and let the law of kindness be in your tongue.
Those who persevere and overcome will have
power over the nations. Abide in Me. Rest in
Me. Run to Me. Hide in Me. Praise Me in all
things. My presence is ever with you. (Read
Matthew 10:8.)

Intercession

**If My people who are called by My name will
humble themselves, and pray and seek My face,
and turn from their wicked ways, then I will
hear from heaven, and will forgive their sin
and heal their land (2 Chronicles 7:14).**

◆

On this Independence Day, I pray for the absolution of our national sins; that virtue in our government and people be strengthened to make clearer strokes across the canvas of time; and that Your name be glorified across the world because of this nation's righteousness. I pray that Jesus Christ so radiantly shine from our lives that darkness and evil will be shoved into oblivion. Let us be a godly nation, known again by Your precious name.

Your intercession is heard and answered. As you pray for world leaders, you will see a difference. Only believing prayer can affect this unseen world where Satan's spiritual forces prey upon the ultimate human authority. *All* eternal victories are won in closets of prayer. (Read 1 Timothy 2:1–2.)

◇

Wait for My Peace

**These things I have spoken to you, that in Me
you may have peace. In the world you will have
tribulation; but be of good cheer, I have
overcome the world (John 16:33).**

◆

*Lord, show us how to live daily in a way that will
make our children and our children's children serve
You, and bring us all to an expected finish, complete
and perfect as You intended from the beginning.*

Commit your way to Me. Trust also in Me.
And I will bring it to pass. That is the only
means by which you bypass those things in life
not chosen by Me. I am a living factor, not just
a positive thought or ideal. The greatest consid-
eration in all your decisions must be Me, your
Heavenly Father. My invitation is always open.
Come in your everyday clothes and we will
search out any perversity or difficulty and un-
ravel it. When you obey Me, My gift is always
peace. If peace does not come, wait. Nothing is
ever lost by waiting. (Read Psalm 37:5.)

Responsibility

**Every good gift and every perfect gift is from
above, and comes down from the Father of
lights, with whom there is no variation
or shadow of turning (James 1:17).**

◆

*Shape me according to Your will, O God. Cause
me to be like You, not how I perceive You to be, but
the way You know Yourself to be.*

Never be satisfied with less. Once you have
had a vision of Me and My thoughts of you, I
will not let you go. Trust Me and I will bring it
to pass. As you believe in accord with My will—
which is always for your benefit—it shall be
done. Bow your head only to Me and take care
that you never bind others to something not ordered by Me. The Holy Spirit at work in your
conscience enables you to do the right thing,
but do not be impatient with another who may
have a different opinion. I always deal with you
in patience, love, and gentleness. (Read Hebrews 12:18–22.)

July 7

◇

Stand and Watch

Do not be overcome by evil, but overcome evil with good (Romans 12:21).

◆

Lord, how can I stand up under criticism when my patience is gone. What am I to do?

There is a term which says: Kill with kindness. As you are gentle, loving, and kind in the face of arrogance, pride, and criticism, your accuser will turn in shame and repent. Stand courageously and trust Me. Watch as I perform the needed surgery to bring that one back to health, a new and shining health that has not yet been experienced. Believe Me. Trust Me. Allow Me. Do not be hurt or rejected or resentful, just patient and peaceful. Keep your eyes on Me. I change not. But I change lives. I love you. (Read Psalm 117:2.)

Idle Thoughts

**I will instruct you and teach you in the way
you should go; I will guide you with
My eye (Psalm 32:8).**

•

*Lord, help me keep my thoughts from floating
about aimlessly . . . jumping the track.*

I will guide you with My eye which is My
set purpose, My will. When you try to jump the
track you are departing from My will. If you per-
sist, you end up derailing. Strange and useless as
any train off the track is your life when you disallow My guidance—power gone, light faded, oil
of the Holy Spirit dried up. Your sadness when
you see a train laid waste can never match the
sadness I feel at one human life wasted for want
of My guidance. Always say, "Yes, Lord," and
remain healthy, cleansed, and purified, deliberately calculating against idle patterns of
thought. Go forth with a robust vigorous confidence . . . on track. (Read Isaiah 55:8–9.)

July 9

◇

I Am God

You shall therefore keep His statutes and His commandments which I command you today, that it may go well with you and with your children after you, and that you may prolong your days in the land which the LORD your God is giving you for all time (Deuteronomy 4:40).

◆

Lord, protect me from the awful, devastating paralysis of sudden fear.

I will drive out the demons from before you, My beloved, and give you their land and space for your inheritance. I am God: there is none else. Keep the statutes and commands that I have spoken to you, that all may go well with you and with your children after you, that your days on earth may be prolonged. Cling not to some natural virtue in yourself which you imagine exists, but rely on My almighty power. Keep your eyes on Me, for it is the vision I give which keeps your spiritual eyesight fresh and vigorous. (Read Romans 12:9.)

Obedience

**The integrity of the upright will guide them,
but the perversity of the unfaithful will
destroy them (Proverbs 11:3).**

♦

*Lord, help me overcome that quick and awful
temptation to defend my position when provoked, criti-
cized, or accused.*

I am your Helper. In returning and rest you
shall be saved; in quietness and confidence shall
be your strength. But the initiative is yours to
cultivate good habits, walk uprightly, and make
the right choices. Be absolutely immediate
when acting on My Word. The way to develop
fine character is so simple: Never hesitate in
choosing My way over temptation. Train your
instincts so that when the crisis comes, there is
no doubt. I will defend you. It is a glorious way
to live. Practice, practice, until it becomes a
habit . . . like taking the next glorious breath.
(Read Philippians 2:13–14.)

Selfless Love

**And we have known and believed the love that
God has for us. God is love, and he who
abides in love abides in God, and
God in him (1 John 4:16).**

❖

*Lord, help us be teachable, so that we will not
need to be brought back through hard lessons again.*

To the degree that pretense is cast aside, you
shall see clearly. You may follow hard after Me
but you shall never reach the goal until you die
to self. My love is all-sufficient. As you make
more room for Me, the lesson becomes clearer
and you begin to love others as I love them, so
that you go forward, not needing to turn to
make repairs. Never allow yourself to fret or be
dismayed. Cultivate love. Water and feed it and
let the roots grow deep. Love is always in season. Learn the lesson of yielding to Me. (Read
1 Timothy 1:5.)

◇

Learn and Conquer

If it is possible, as much as depends on you, live peaceably with all men (Romans 12:18).

◆

Lord, keep hurtful situations from turning into mountains. Help me make peace with grace and ease, patience, fearlessness, and an ear for Your voice.

The more conscious of Me you become, the more peacemaking becomes simple, easy, practical. If you would be patient, learn to welcome interruption. To be comfortable with yourself and others, learn humility. To overcome selfishness, practice giving and learn to enjoy menial tasks. If you would conquer fear, meditate on the courage of Jesus. To overcome any lack, worship and praise Me. If you desire to hear My voice perfectly, purify yourself, confess, repent, and listen. My Spirit speaks as softly as the balmy desert breeze. But remember, My revelation to you is determined by your character and not by Mine. (Read Acts 24:16 and 1 Thessalonians 5:18.)

Satan: Master of Disguise

Behold, I give you the authority to trample on
serpents and scorpions, and over all the power
of the enemy, and nothing shall by any
means hurt you (Luke 10:19).

◆

*Lord, my bones are heavy and my shoulders are
tensed as though I'd never slept. I feel sick all over.*

Do not be deceived! Satan is an illusion
maker . . . a master of disguise. He erects barricades in your path that are not real. But you see
them as real, and react accordingly. Do not see
with your earthly senses, but see with the eyes
of the Spirit. Stand on My most holy Word:
Nothing shall by any means harm you. You are
Mine, child of the King! Do not sign for Satan's
delivery. Immediately speak against it! And the
enemy will take it elsewhere. Fear not! For I am
the Lord who keeps you. (Read 1 Peter 5:8.)

Perfect Answers

His divine power has given to us all things
that pertain to life and godliness, through
the knowledge of Him who called us
by glory and virtue (2 Peter 1:3).

◆

Lord, help me to abdicate power. Keep my mind
with an eagerness for Your almighty control.

You used to seek your own counsel, faulty
was. By now you know that you will never
k of anything I have forgotten. I have an-
s that are uniquely perfect for each situa-
. Rest in that confidence. Never declare that
e is not enough! Banish self-pity and doubt
re they assassinate Me and raise your selfish-
to the throne. There is nothing lovely in
murmurings of the greedy. If My majesty
grace and power are not living in you, you
responsible, not I. *Receive* My nature. I am
haddai, the God of Plenty. (Read Matthew
and Psalm 130:7.)

Power to Be Silent

Be still, and know that I am God; I will
be exalted among the nations, I will be
exalted in the earth! (Psalm 46:10).

◆

Lord, help us lay down our prejudices. Use Your
bright shining to purify us inwardly so that we may
live up to the vision You have of us.

I come so gently, and speak so softly. Let
drop away any concern, anything, or anybody
that obscures the vision of your conscience.
Wait and renew the spirit of your mind. Being
still before Me is never a waste. In faith and in
quietness is your strength. The sunshine makes
no noise but it is so powerful that without it life
on earth would cease. Be still, and know that I
am God! Receive power to be silent. (Read 1 Peter 3:3–4.)

◇

Pride

Blessed are those whose lawless deeds are forgiven, and whose sins are covered (Romans 4:7).

◆

Lord, I have failed so miserably. Visions of my flaws and lack of grace are ever before my eyes.

My child, pride causes you to criticize yourself and hold on to defeat and failure, just as surely as ego causes you to hold a past victory ever before your eyes. When I make provision for your forgiveness and healing, it is not lack of faith that makes you fail to receive My grace but arrogance and rebellion. I say, receive. Lay your pride on the altar and I will consume it. Then go forward unafraid, free to be kind and loving with your words, your acts, your eyes. Forgiving yourself as I have forgiven you; expecting neither restitution nor punishment. Not wallowing in guilt but walking in liberty. For there is no condemnation in Christ Jesus. (Read Romans 8:1.)

◇

No Compla[...]

**Rejoice always, pray wit[...]
(1 Thessalonians 5:1[...]**

◆

Lord, save me from irritat[...] ableness; help me to say, no matt[...] am delighted to obey You in this [...]

First, never give way to self-[...] It makes one unfit for My Wo[...] to be alive and active in you al[...] always remember why you are s[...] Son of God might be manifes[...] your tongue, your brain, and yo[...] rest. Let no whine or misery be[...] No complaining! Jesus never co[...] *rested* and *waited* for My will. Ev[...] life that is of any value you owe [...] tion. Rejoice always, and again I[...] thankful always. As you thank[...] many blessings, it will infect eve[...] life with the same grateful spirit. [...] harmony with My Spirit, your m[...] the world. (Read 1 John 3:5.)

Humility

Yet indeed I also count all things loss for the excellence of the knowledge of Christ Jesus my Lord, for whom I have suffered the loss of all things, and count them as rubbish, that I may gain Christ and be found in Him, not having my own righteousness, which is from the law, but that which is through faith in Christ, the righteousness which is from God by faith (Philippians 3:8–9).

◆

When I look at the stormy weather of many lives, then at my own, I know it is Your grace at work, Lord. Show me the fast You have chosen this month.

My grace is a gift that exhibits to others My power to keep. Be watchful lest pride should enter. Remember that the underside of your strength is weakness. Never glory in yourself. Better to say, "There but for God's grace go I. I delight to obey You, Lord. Do with me as You will." Let this fast be not from food but rather from preaching, from an attitude of criticism, from self. (Read Matthew 7:1–2.)

July 19

◇

Obedience

You call Me Teacher and Lord, and you say well, for so I am (John 13:13).

◆

O Master, I seem so slow to learn. Show me the secret way to "delight" in obeying You.

Your growth in grace comes according to the way you view obedience. True obedience is only possible between those of equal wills . . . with freedom to choose. Jesus did not obey in order to "become"; He obeyed because He already was My Son. I never insist. But I tell you softly that marvelous things occur when My people decide on a steadfast, unflinching course to conquer self. Spiritual power is the outworking of inward denial and obedience. Remember, My child, I make all things work together for your good. Trust Me. (Read 1 Peter 1:22.)

Walk in the Light

**But if we walk in the light as He is in the light,
we have fellowship with one another, and the
blood of Jesus Christ His Son cleanses
us from all sin (1 John 1:7).**

♦

*Help us, O God, to follow after You and not after
the fallen Adam who blamed his wife for his sin; nor
after Eve, who blamed the beguiling deception of Satan. Help us to live honestly, with simplicity, not hiding from You nor deceiving ourselves.*

Be as little children. Walk in the light. Follow My advice to the smallest detail, for only I
know completely and consider every facet of
your individual personality, character, capability, and circumstance. Hidden lives and spiritual
failure often come by undisciplined natures—
after Satan has already been defeated. Be quiet
in your mind and listen to Me. Your character
shall change, your strength and power be renewed as you wait. (Read Isaiah 40:31.)

◇

Deliverance

Rejoice in the LORD, you righteous, and give
thanks at the remembrance of His
holy name (Psalm 97:12).

♦

*Precious Father, I feel like a whining complainer
this morning. Give me directions out of this place.*

Speak to that mountain in soft murmurings
of thankfulness, shout "grace," and sing songs
of praise and adoration. As your tongue con-
fesses righteous, faith-filled thoughts, you will
be enabled to watch the mountain dissolve. Let
no worry or concern hinder your progress. Let
no accusation or rejection get you down. I am
still on My throne. I will never let you go. And
when you fail, be not defeated. All you need do
is confess, repent, and receive forgiveness, then
go forward unafraid. It is so simple; yet even My
most mature followers miss it at times and take
on the burden of failure. Learn how to receive
fully . . . instantly. Be filled up with thankfulness and joy. It is the sure path of deliverance.
(Read Zechariah 4:7.)

Power to Be Silent

**Be still, and know that I am God; I will
be exalted among the nations, I will be
exalted in the earth! (Psalm 46:10).**

◆

*Lord, help us lay down our prejudices. Use Your
bright shining to purify us inwardly so that we may
live up to the vision You have of us.*

I come so gently, and speak so softly. Let
drop away any concern, anything, or anybody
that obscures the vision of your conscience.
Wait and renew the spirit of your mind. Being
still before Me is never a waste. In faith and in
quietness is your strength. The sunshine makes
no noise but it is so powerful that without it life
on earth would cease. Be still, and know that I
am God! Receive power to be silent. (Read 1 Peter 3:3–4.)

◇

Pride

**Blessed are those whose lawless deeds
are forgiven, and whose sins are
covered (Romans 4:7).**

◆

*Lord, I have failed so miserably. Visions of my
flaws and lack of grace are ever before my eyes.*

My child, pride causes you to criticize yourself and hold on to defeat and failure, just as surely as ego causes you to hold a past victory ever before your eyes. When I make provision for your forgiveness and healing, it is not lack of faith that makes you fail to receive My grace but arrogance and rebellion. I say, receive. Lay your pride on the altar and I will consume it. Then go forward unafraid, free to be kind and loving with your words, your acts, your eyes. Forgiving yourself as I have forgiven you; expecting neither restitution nor punishment. Not wallowing in guilt but walking in liberty. For there is no condemnation in Christ Jesus. (Read Romans 8:1.)

No Complaining

**Rejoice always, pray without ceasing
(1 Thessalonians 5:16–17).**

◆

*Lord, save me from irritation and disagree-
ableness; help me to say, no matter what, "Lord, I
am delighted to obey You in this matter."*

First, never give way to self-pity. It is deadly.
It makes one unfit for My Word, which needs
to be alive and active in you always. You must
always remember why you are saved, so that the
Son of God might be manifested in you. Let
your tongue, your brain, and your nerves be at
rest. Let no whine or misery be found in you.
No complaining! Jesus never complained, but
rested and *waited* for My will. Every bit of your
life that is of any value you owe to His redemption. Rejoice always, and again I say rejoice! Be
thankful always. As you thank Me for your
many blessings, it will infect everyone in your
life with the same grateful spirit. As you sing in
harmony with My Spirit, your music will thrill
the world. (Read 1 John 3:5.)

July 17

Perfect Answers

As His divine power has given to us all things
that pertain to life and godliness, through
the knowledge of Him who called us
by glory and virtue (2 Peter 1:3).

◆

*Lord, help me to abdicate power. Keep my mind
filled with an eagerness for Your almighty control.*

You used to seek your own counsel, faulty
as it was. By now you know that you will never
think of anything I have forgotten. I have answers that are uniquely perfect for each situation. Rest in that confidence. Never declare that
there is not enough! Banish self-pity and doubt
before they assassinate Me and raise your selfishness to the throne. There is nothing lovely in
the murmurings of the greedy. If My majesty
and grace and power are not living in you, you
are responsible, not I. *Receive* My nature. I am
El Shaddai, the God of Plenty. (Read Matthew
7:11 and Psalm 130:7.)

Humility

Yet indeed I also count all things loss for the excellence of the knowledge of Christ Jesus my Lord, for whom I have suffered the loss of all things, and count them as rubbish, that I may gain Christ and be found in Him, not having my own righteousness, which is from the law, but that which is through faith in Christ, the righteousness which is from God by faith (Philippians 3:8–9).

◆

When I look at the stormy weather of many lives, then at my own, I know it is Your grace at work, Lord. Show me the fast You have chosen this month.

My grace is a gift that exhibits to others My power to keep. Be watchful lest pride should enter. Remember that the underside of your strength is weakness. Never glory in yourself. Better to say, "There but for God's grace go I. I delight to obey You, Lord. Do with me as You will." Let this fast be not from food but rather from preaching, from an attitude of criticism, from self. (Read Matthew 7:1–2.)

◇

Obedience

**You call Me Teacher and Lord, and you say
well, for so I am (John 13:13).**

◆

*O Master, I seem so slow to learn. Show me the
secret way to "delight" in obeying You.*

Your growth in grace comes according to the
way you view obedience. True obedience is only
possible between those of equal wills . . . with
freedom to choose. Jesus did not obey in order
to "become"; He obeyed because He already
was My Son. I never insist. But I tell you softly
that marvelous things occur when My people
decide on a steadfast, unflinching course to conquer self. Spiritual power is the outworking of
inward denial and obedience. Remember, My
child, I make all things work together for your
good. Trust Me. (Read 1 Peter 1:22.)

Walk in the Light

**But if we walk in the light as He is in the light,
we have fellowship with one another, and the
blood of Jesus Christ His Son cleanses
us from all sin (1 John 1:7).**

♦

*Help us, O God, to follow after You and not after
the fallen Adam who blamed his wife for his sin; nor
after Eve, who blamed the beguiling deception of Satan. Help us to live honestly, with simplicity, not hiding from You nor deceiving ourselves.*

Be as little children. Walk in the light. Follow My advice to the smallest detail, for only I
know completely and consider every facet of
your individual personality, character, capability, and circumstance. Hidden lives and spiritual
failure often come by undisciplined natures—
after Satan has already been defeated. Be quiet
in your mind and listen to Me. Your character
shall change, your strength and power be renewed as you wait. (Read Isaiah 40:31.)

Deliverance

Rejoice in the LORD, you righteous, and give
thanks at the remembrance of His
holy name (Psalm 97:12).

◆

*Precious Father, I feel like a whining complainer
this morning. Give me directions out of this place.*

Speak to that mountain in soft murmurings
of thankfulness, shout "grace," and sing songs
of praise and adoration. As your tongue con-
fesses righteous, faith-filled thoughts, you will
be enabled to watch the mountain dissolve. Let
no worry or concern hinder your progress. Let
no accusation or rejection get you down. I am
still on My throne. I will never let you go. And
when you fail, be not defeated. All you need do
is confess, repent, and receive forgiveness, then
go forward unafraid. It is so simple; yet even My
most mature followers miss it at times and take
on the burden of failure. Learn how to receive
fully . . . instantly. Be filled up with thankfulness and joy. It is the sure path of deliverance.
(Read Zechariah 4:7.)

Full Provision

**For whoever desires to save his life will lose it,
but whoever loses his life for My sake
will save it (Luke 9:24).**

◆

*O Lord, I pray that we may walk in habitual
fellowship with You, experiencing that real life which
only You can give.*

Then cast out all doubt and throw off all
limitations for I have said, "Ask what you will
and it shall be done unto you." You have a marvelous future with My unlimited power to bless
others. Let no fear, depression, moodiness, selfishness, critical attitude, or lack of any kind be
a part of your thinking. I want life for My children—ready for death of self, but eager for Me.
Be willing to be stripped of all that is not really
you, of all your friends think of you, the impression you hope to make, all you think of yourself
(good or bad); then receive total purity because
I am pure and dwell within you. Receive life!
Cherish real life! (Read Genesis 6:3 and John
17:20–21.)

Faith

But without faith it is impossible to please Him, for he who comes to God must believe that He is, and that He is a rewarder of those who diligently seek Him (Hebrews 11:6).

◆

Lord, clear the confusion and give us Your peace.

Only when you put something or someone before Me is there confusion and lack of peace. Worry and pressure are never right, for such emotions indicate you do not think I can take care of the details of your life. Lack of faith is infidelity. Without faith you cannot please Me. The cares of the world choke My Word. It is a sickness. Lean on Me, My children. Oh, when will you learn that I am here for all things, to bear the small burdens as well as the large. Trust Me. Rely on and cling to Me. I am all you need. Let the perfection and holiness of My Son, Jesus, be manifest in your flesh. Christ in you, by faith, a sovereign gift of My grace and indisputable order. (Read Matthew 13:22.)

◇

Live in My Presence

**Depart from evil and do good; seek peace
and pursue it (Psalm 34:14).**

◆

*Lord Jesus, let Your virtue flow . . . that we may
receive healing for our bodies . . . and glorify You.*

Covet My will. Your own way will turn on
you and pierce and splinter you. My way will
protect and guide you to victory. Think, act,
and live in My presence—the secret of all health,
all power, all peace, all purity, all influence.
These virtues no man can take from you, and
no one has the power to disturb or steal. But
you forfeit peace by allowing in the world's cares
and distractions. Only you can open the door
to fear and despondency, or to the thief who
would destroy your health and rob you of
power, purity, and influence. Set yourselves.
Allow *nothing* to disturb your calm. Kill irritation and annoyance. Do not hesitate! Do not
entertain these evil enemies for an instant. (Read
Colossians 3:2 and Romans 8:11.)

Blessed Are the Meek

**Is this not the fast that I have chosen: to loose
the bonds of wickedness, to undo the heavy
burdens, to let the oppressed go free, and
that you break every yoke? (Isaiah 58:6).**

●

*Bless this fast, O God. Let our traditional way of
settling disputes be broken. Stop us from putting forth
fingers of criticism and speaking empty, selfish words.
Heal us, heal our bodies, Lord.*

The fast I have chosen breaks every yoke,
looses from wickedness, frees from burdens and
completely quenches the enemy's fire. The fast
makes it easier to see another's nakedness.
When you cover others while building up your
own waste places, you will be known as a re-
pairer and restorer. And your light shall spring
forth as the morning and your health shall
speedily return. "Blessed are the peacemakers"
is simple to interpret but it takes a stern discipline to receive My Spirit's execution in the
midst of a situation where self wants its own
way. (Read Isaiah 58:7–12.)

Purity

**Bless the LORD, O my soul; and all that is
within me, bless His holy name! Bless the
LORD, O my soul, and forget not all
His benefits (Psalm 103:1–2).**

◆

*Great Shepherd, guide me through the water.
Strengthen me through this time of discipline.*

Everyone who asks receives. Not sometime
but every time. Always in the best way. Recognize that I am the supreme authority of the human heart and be not resentful over what I
reveal there. Instantly own up to sin, finding no
refuge in innocence, which is a child's characteristic and not to be confused with purity. Purity,
as it was in Jesus, is wrought with full knowledge of good and evil, by the Holy Spirit. It is
only since you turned your heart over to Me
that your attraction to sin has diminished, for I
give you power to lead a blameless life. I direct
you, crown your efforts with success, and renew
your health, youth, and vitality. (Read Psalm
103:3–4; 1 Thessalonians 5:23.)

Know My Voice

My voice You shall hear in the morning,
O LORD; in the morning I will direct it
to You, and I will look up (Psalm 5:3).

◆

*Father, help me to be as a little child, listening,
knowing Your voice as I know my earthly father's.*

I will never tell you anything which will cause hurt or destruction. My voice instructs you always toward peaceable solutions—building up some walls, tearing down others. When you know My voice you cannot be led into a thicket of brambles from which it would be hard to extricate yourself. And I will warn you when your tender conscience threatens to become a weight and a hindrance. Let your own voice speak with wisdom and let the law of kindness be in your tongue, spawning health and making glad a heavy, stooping heart. Let love be your constant guide. Listen! and take care not to allow another voice to steal from you this day. Rejoice! This is the day that I have made. (Read John 10:27.)

Live Today

The LORD is my strength and my shield; my
heart trusted in Him, and I am helped;
therefore my heart greatly rejoices, and with
my song I will praise Him (Psalm 28:7).

♦

*What a God You are! Perfect in every way. A
shield for everyone who hides behind You. You give me
the surefootedness of a goat, leading me safely along
the precipice, preparing me for battle and giving me
strength to draw an iron bow. Hallelujah! You have
made wide steps beneath my feet so that I need never
slip or stumble. You have armed me with strong
armor and weapons. Intellectually, I know Your
promises are all true. Yet sometimes I feel afraid. Help
me to know the battle is not mine but Yours, O Lord.*

Fear not! I *am* your shield. See me standing
between you and all harm. My resurrection life
makes perfect harmony possible. Remember
that to Me, the process is the goal. My training
is for today. And each moment is precious. Practice obedience today! (Read 2 Chronicles 20:17
and Acts 5:29.)

My Will Is Clear

Jesus said to them, "My food is to do the will of Him who sent Me, and to finish His work" (John 4:34).

◆

Dear Lord, be the umpire of our decisions. Let Your will be a clear shining to us, and not clouded.

My will is always clear. Don't concern yourself with clouds, for by them you are taught to walk by faith. No clouds, no faith! Look upon them as a sign that I am here. Look on even the darkest, most thunderous clouds with perfect belief, and let them not in any way affect your faith . . . or impugn My character. Maintain an undisturbed relationship with Me. When you leave the choosing to Me, I pick a way through the bleak terrain that has colorful flowers, lovely butterflies, sunny glades, and fresh summer air. (Read Colossians 3:15.)

Heed My Directions

To console those who mourn in Zion, to give
them beauty for ashes, the oil of joy for
mourning, the garment of praise for the spirit
of heaviness; that they may be called trees of
righteousness, the planting of the LORD,
that He may be glorified (Isaiah 61:3).

◆

*Why do we see such crime, Lord; why are families
being destroyed; and why is society on the verge of col-
lapse? How will we explain it to our children?*

Tell them it is because My laws have been
broken. Man has not heeded the directions I
gave for a healthy society. Since man's tongue
and his doings are against Me, their children re-
bel and behave criminally even against the aged;
the treacherous cheat and debase their employ-
ers, the government, and the honorable. But
should I change the laws of nature to accommo-
date the whims of man? No! They who turn
back to Me shall be instantly saved and forgiven.
They shall receive beauty for ashes and joy for
mourning. (Read Proverbs 4:13.)

◇

Purity

**For with God nothing will be
impossible (Luke 1:37).**

◆

*My Lord, if I have found favor in Your sight, do
not pass me by . . . heal my body altogether.*

Is anything too hard or too wonderful for
Me? Look for Me in every happening. I am the
real cause for joy and gratitude. Every detail of
your life is under My scrutiny and I make all
things work together for your good. Examine
yourself for unfinished places. Your notice shall
be brought to those places again and again until
the rough edges become smooth. Trust not in
yourself to accomplish the task but in My grace.
When My requirements have been met I will
send you to fill the needs of others. Allow Me
to transfigure you by My indwelling life. Be
changed easily! Think on only good things,
speak only good, and let your ears transmit positive impulses to your body. Let your reactions
to what you hear be pure: Be healed! (Read Romans 8:28 and Philippians 4:8.)

August

My beloved brethren, let every
man be swift to hear, slow to
speak, slow to wrath.

James 1:19

Fear

Peace I leave with you, My peace I give to you;
not as the world gives do I give to you. Let
not your heart be troubled, neither let
it be afraid (John 14:27).

•

*Dear Father, I am a coward. As much so as the
disciples who ran away when Jesus was taken prisoner.
I lack courage, which is a hard thing for me to admit,
but through Your grace I see and can confess it. I lack
the courage to suffer, the courage to face malignancy,
to lose my life. I want to keep all that makes life worth
living: my husband, our children and grandchildren,
our plans for the future, my work. I want more of
You, more of life. And I am afraid of bearing the
cross . . . as cowardly as Peter who denied You. Father,
I know not how to endure a doctor's unfavorable report, but I know You'll make me strong and pull me
through. You know what I can bear. I know Your love
will be with me, for in Your plan, suffering is not the
end.*

Be not afraid, My child. I have overcome the
world! (Read John 16:33.)

Fear

**You are of God, little children, and have
overcome them, because He who is in
you is greater than he who is in
the world (1 John 4:4).**

◆

*. . . And yet I am afraid, Father. Afraid of the
unknown.*

You shall not fear Satan's lies nor his damnable spirits. For I, your Lord Jesus, have overcome every work of hell, even death. Fear is Satan's most evil ally. To be afraid is to give him a place to stand. And he is a liar, deceiver, illusion-builder, manipulator, and destroyer. Listen not to his lies! Sacrifice not yourself at his altar, not the tiniest portion of your thought life; neither allow your brow to frown nor your back to bend under any yoke of oppression. Hear Me alone! Praise My truth. Have reverence for Me. Bow yourself for My blessing. I give you power and love and a sound, alert, undefaced mind . . . Mine! (Read John 8:44.)

August 3

◇

Youthful Vitality

Bless the LORD, O my soul; and all that is
within me, bless His holy name! . . . who
satisfies your mouth with good things,
so that your youth is renewed like
the eagle's (Psalm 103:1, 5).

◆

*My Lord and my God, if You left me alone from
this day forward, You have already done far more
than I deserve. Although I love Your justice, I am
grateful far more for Your mercy, for that is what I
need. Your unmerited favor has spared me. I could
have been destroyed for lack of knowledge, but Your
love and the never-ending intercession and self-
sacrifice of Your Son, Jesus, brought me to this place.*

I know how you can best be used, guided
by your ordinary choices, and checked if you are
about to make a wrong decision. Stop and listen
as I share with you My secrets and joys. Be silent. Give Me your thoughts. I call you to raise
up that youth that is in you. Let vitality burst
forth as a spring morning. I am preparing you
for a new vision. (Read Hosea 4:6.)

Guidance

Come, you children, listen to me; I will teach
you the fear of the LORD. Who is the man who
desires life, and loves many days, that he may
see good? Keep your tongue from evil, and
your lips from speaking deceit. Depart
from evil and do good; seek peace
and pursue it (Psalm 34:11–4).

♦

*Lord, show us the door of hope where we can stand
and sing of Your love with a full, hearty sound.*

My children, come and listen and let Me
teach you the importance of trusting and fearing
Me, your Master. Do you want a long, good
life? Then watch your tongue! Keep your lips
from lying. Turn from all known sin and spend
the days and nights, hours and moments thinking and doing good. Live in peace with everyone. My eyes are intently watching all who live
good lives, and I give My attention when they
cry to Me. My angels guard the door of hope
and rescue those who revere Me. (Read Exodus
23:20.)

August 5

◇

Seek Me Always

Yet I am the LORD your God ever since the land of Egypt, and you shall know no God but Me; for there is no savior besides Me (Hosea 13:4).

◆

Lord, help me to bury fear, apprehension, dread, and cowardice permanently.

Your need is My summons. I will ransom you from the power of the grave. Do not fear the plague and pestilence. Wait on Me, for there is no Savior besides Me. They that dwell in My shadow shall be revived and grow as the vine and blossom, and the fragrance shall be as a fine wine. As long as you seek Me, I will make you prosper, build you up, and repair your wounds. And when you are strong, do not cut yourself off from Me as some do when the catastrophe is past. Keep your heart centered on Me, praising Me always for the great things I have done for you. (Read Hosea 14:7.)

Empowerment

I can of Myself do nothing. As I hear, I judge;
and My judgment is righteous, because I do
not seek My own will but the will of the
Father who sent Me (John 5:30).

◆

*Lord, help us make ordinary choices that are Your
choices, as naturally as we choose to take the next
breath.*

Whatever it is that stands between the will
and the doing is sin, that perverse human disposition. The unintelligence that refuses to be en-
lightened. This trait can only be destroyed by
inviting the Holy Spirit to crowd into your
mind and heart and make you obedient. Quietly
commune with Me—away, alone—without
noise and activity in the secret place of the Most
High, and you will leave that encounter with
power to bless and heal and deliver. Power to
make right decisions. Power to be creative. My
power. (Read 1 Chronicles 28:9.)

◇

Spirit of Worry

**Every word of God is pure; He is a shield
to those who put their trust in Him
(Proverbs 30:5).**

◆

*Lord, Help me to recognize Your power at the very
outset of fear or doubt.*

Never allow fear a place. Fear is of Satan and
not of Me. I am greater than any trouble you
can have. Whatever you expect from Me will
happen! The children of Israel truly believed
that all would be dreadful and they would perish
in the wilderness. Exactly as their mistrust and
worrying spirit declared, it came to pass. But
those who *trusted* Me and said that I would sustain them found that I did. They took posses-
sion of the Promised Land. Be secure. Roll all
your cares onto Me. And let your face be clear,
joyful, and serene. (Read 1 Peter 5:7–8; Philippians 4:6–7; Job 3:25.)

Security

For He Himself is our peace, who has made both one, and has broken down the middle wall of separation (Ephesians 2:14).

◆

Lord, show me how to depend on You completely.

Shove yourself away from the safety of what you hold onto for security. Everyone is clamoring for security . . . for peace. I am your security. I am your peace. Make room within you for quiet, holy communion with Me. Let My virtue mellow you and make you ripe. Give Me the moments of which I have spoken to you so often. Receive My love. (Read 2 Thessalonians 3:16.)

August 9

◇

Security

**Praise the LORD! Praise the LORD, O my soul!
While I live I will praise the LORD; I will
sing praises to my God while I have
my being (Psalm 146:1–2).**

◆

*Lord, I seek a deep dwelling . . . a safe path. And
true, natural thankfulness.*

True praise is a worthy sacrifice. This really
honors Me. And when you trust Me and walk
My path, you give Me pleasure. Fear adds not
one millimeter to your protection of yourself.
Trust Me . . . and be fearless. My blessing is rich
and I add no sorrow to it. I am your security
blanket. Still your begging, and quietly trust.
(Read Proverbs 10:22.)

Choose My Will

**Then Jacob awoke from his sleep and said,
"Surely the LORD is in this place, and I
did not know it" (Genesis 28:16).**

◆

*Lord, wherever I am today help me say, as Jacob
said, "Surely the Lord is in this place."*

The brightness of My glory is truly round
about you. Receive My peace, heartrest, and
comfort amidst agitation, confusion, and suffering. My angelic beings stand beside you to but-
tress, protect, and minister to you. Seek out and
concentrate on the greater vision. Let your gaze
stay on the goal and not every bypass and sign-
post along the way. (Read Matthew 16:23 and
Philippians 3:13–14.)

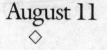

August 11

◇

Cling to Me

**Therefore by Him let us continually offer the
sacrifice of praise to God, that is, the fruit
of our lips, giving thanks to His name
(Hebrews 13:15).**

♦

*Lord, refresh us this day with the oil of Your Holy
Spirit to fuel our flames of praise.*

Sin and sorrow and repression cease where
the song of praise commences. Turn to Me.
Cling to Me. Therein lies the answer to all.
Stubbornness of heart will keep you from rest;
or render you unwilling when I call you from
frailty and exhaustion. When you come to your
Red Sea or your Jordan, put into practice what
you have learned from your Lord, your Elijah,
your prophet: Repent. Believe. Praise. Worship.
(Read Psalm 100:2.)

Prayer

Therefore I exhort first of all that supplications, prayers, intercessions, and giving of thanks be made for all men (1 Timothy 2:1).

◆

Dear Lord, help us to live daily as if our dearest, closest love had told us in great detail how to live and be happy and to have eternal life.

Live in a large sense. Change whatever is wrong by prayer and intercession. Think My thoughts and not your own, for your thoughts are weak and hopeless, while Mine are power-filled, confident, absolutely right, and loving. Let Me be everything to you. I am closer than your next thought. (Read Proverbs 18:24.)

Live Now

**For you were once darkness, but now you are
light in the Lord. Walk as children of
light (Ephesians 5:8).**

◆

*Precious Father, thank You for preserving us, our
family, our possessions, and for returning us home
safely.*

I am your provision, your hidden manna,
and your protector all the day long. How often
tragedy and disappointment would strike except
by My grace. Walk in the light, My children,
and in wonder of this *present* moment. Not in
memory and not for tomorrow. Now! When a
crisis point comes, go through it boldly, then
on to the next. Do not get stuck on anything—
learn it now, so that you will not have to repeat
it. Let your life be a holy experiment, always creative and original, never stagnant. Always fed by
Me. I am perennially fresh. Live *now!* (Read Revelation 2:17.)

Serenity

**For you died, and your life is hidden with
Christ in God (Colossians 3:3).**

◆

Lord, Lord, make me think like You.

No, you have to do that yourself. Bring
every thought into captivity as did the obedient
Christ. Abide in Me, in all things, casting down
all imaginings. Wherever your body happens to
be, you can be in as close communion with Me
as if you were in a dynamic prayer meeting. Yet
you do not have to be kept at a high pitch of
excitement. Look at Jesus! Where is the serenity
of the life hid with Christ in God about you?
Serenity is a continual effort until it becomes a
habit. But it begins by bringing the thoughts
into captivity . . . where I can begin to purify
you wholly . . . which is the goal . . . to make
you holy as I am holy. Take your eyes off the
petty; embrace the greater vision; and you will
begin to think like Me. (Read 1 Peter 1:13–15.)

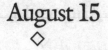

◇

Discipline

And do not be conformed to this world, but be transformed by the renewing of your mind, that you may prove what is that good and acceptable and perfect will of God (Romans 12:2).

◆

Wonderful Savior, I want to look forward with sweet expectation and stirring hope to these times with You, and not consider them a matter of drudgery.

Then pay attention. Diligently concentrate. Right thinking is patiently constructed. Begin with small things and it will become routine. It is discipline that keeps you between the times of soaring inspiration. Take the words I speak each day and do what I tell you. Only then can I show you the next step. Please. What must I do to have you see that the *now*, the present moment is so very important to Me. I know you *want* My will, yet you struggle so to *do* it. Rest in My presence, let Me fill you. Let your thoughts not run away but bring them back to Me. You are learning! (Read Colossians 3:16.)

Comfort

**Blessed be the God and Father of our Lord
Jesus Christ, the Father of mercies and God
of all comfort, who comforts us in all our
tribulation, that we may be able to comfort
those who are in any trouble, with the comfort
with which we ourselves are comforted
by God (2 Corinthians 1:3–4).**

◆

Thank You, sweet Lord, for comforting us, assuring us, releasing us, purifying us.

I want you to know how much I love you.
I will strengthen you to do all that you need to
do. I will give you courage to overcome,
strength to persevere, and victory over anything
the enemy throws at you. I am the Father of
mercies and the God of all comfort, who comforts you in all your tribulation, that you may
be able to comfort others the same way you have
been comforted. (Read 1 Thessalonians 5:11.)

◇

Self-Criticism

**There is therefore now no condemnation to
those who are in Christ Jesus (Romans 8:1).**

◆

Lord, help me to be stubborn in my believing, while I go to war against self-criticism, self-condemnation, and guilt.

If you would live as I live, you would walk in the light of brilliant moments in quite ordinary ways. It is a difficult thing, for the human nature rebels and defends and wants its credit. But I call you to put away those selfish departures, while avoiding any critical temper toward yourself when you fail. Self-criticism keeps you analyzing your behavior from moment to moment, measuring and dividing, weighing and wondering. Centered on self, you entrap yourself into defiance or discouragement. When you fall short, remember My redemption and be gloriously happy. Simply say, "Lord, I'm sorry," and I will satisfy you with My forgiveness. But you must *forgive yourself!* (Read Ephesians 1:7.)

Courage

Have I not commanded you? Be strong and of good courage; do not be afraid, nor be dismayed, for the LORD your God is with you wherever you go (Joshua 1:9).

◆

Lord, quiet my soul. Lift the veil from my eyes. I am working hard at not being afraid of what lies ahead.

Be strong and courageous. Be not afraid nor dismayed, for I am with you wherever you go. There is more with you than is against you, if you can see with spiritual eyes. You have the Lord and Creator of all space, and all that fills that space. I am the God of the microcosm as well as the macrocosm. Believe not the arrogant claims of the enemy when he tries to persuade you that your trust in Me is misplaced, or tempts you, or tries to shame you with suggestions that your God is too small. Be not afraid. My angels surround you. (Read Psalm 91:11–12.)

Self-Scrutiny

Thus says the LORD: "Stand in the ways and see, and ask for the old paths, where the good way is, and walk in it; then you will find rest for your souls. But they said, 'We will not walk in it'" (Jeremiah 6:16).

◆

Lord, our longing is to become the disciples of passionate devotion You have purposed us to be.

Jesus' devotion and obedience was first to My will, and then to the needs of men. There is an order: devotion, obedience, then ministry. Self-consciousness is the cause of sketchy love and obedience. The only cure for it is Christ-consciousness. If you do not face the situation, it will keep recurring every time you find yourself in new circumstances. Self-scrutiny caused Peter to fall into the water; "Jesus-scrutiny" caused him to walk on top of it. Recklessly launch out when I speak. Will to do My will without hesitation, for that is where the battle is fought, in the arena of the will. (Read Romans 6:6–8 and Matthew 14:28–31.)

The Secret of Ease

Therefore humble yourselves under the mighty hand of God, that He may exalt you in due time (1 Peter 5:6).

◆

O Lord, give me an easy way to be at ease, ruling my spirit, controlling my mind and emotions, letting my body rest, moving through the days with poise and grace. Protect me from the tyranny of the urgent. Show me how to defend myself.

Be as a little child. Make appointments but be unconcerned over them, or the many chores of the day. An obedient child hears and follows a parent's command through to accomplishment. The secret of "ease" is keeping in touch with Me. Wherever I am, there is rest. Wherever I am, activity is perfected. No frantic racing or urgent seeking, no worry or stress. Simplicity comes by practice—gradual and patient practice. Bring your thoughts into captivity until it becomes routine, an act unconscious of itself. Always trusting, peaceful, unrushed. (Read Proverbs 25:28.)

August 21

◇

Unaffected Loneliness

Commit your way to the LORD, trust also in Him, and He shall bring it to pass (Psalm 37:5).

◆

Lord, when will I cease this feeling of interrupted communication with You?

Launch out in reckless belief that your redemption is complete and stop re-searching the inside to see what is yet unredeemed. Strength and beauty of character come as you yield to Me! As that strong belief and unaffected loveliness is established between us, there shall rush forth from you rivers of living water. But if you pause to examine the flow, it stops, frozen at the point of inspection. (Read Acts 17:28.)

◇

Holiness

Therefore you shall be perfect, just as your Father in heaven is perfect (Matthew 5:48).

◆

Lord, give me something special, meaningful, and current for my life today!

Be ye perfect even as your Father in heaven is perfect—perfect for your stage of development. Present yourself whole and pure as a habit. Build yourself up by feasting on My Word. You have become barren through busyness and, therefore, find Me difficult to reach. I am here! Wait in My presence for a new touch of fire in your soul, a new anointing. Repentance precedes all faith. Surprise Me with the kind of faith where you totally throw yourself on Me, your Lord, as your only hope. Surrender your self-will many times a day. Holiness (My wholeness) cannot come until selfish pride is dead. (Read Leviticus 11:44–45.)

August 23

◇

Sleep That Restores

It is vain for you to rise up early, to sit up late, to eat the bread of sorrows; for so He gives His beloved sleep (Psalm 127:2).

◆

Lord, thank You for Your gift of sleep. Rule our dreams and reveal Your great thoughts to us through them.

Sleep well, My child, for it is indeed your friend. Sleep as a child sleeps, trusting Me for its care, receiving strength indefatigable to start afresh every morning and carry on until nap time. A child knows how to put off what he has to do until tomorrow. Mind you, to the sluggard I would have a different message. Don't think, however, that laziness is a greater sin than restlessness, for it is not. The lazy lack courage to work. The restless lack the courage to be inactive. Stretch out. Rest. Sleep. Be at peace. It is good to trust in One whose eyes are always open. It is good to be silent. Let sleep restore you. (Read Proverbs 3:24.)

Faith

Jesus said to him, "If you can believe, all things are possible to him who believes" (Mark 9:23).

♦

Lord, my God, my enlightenment, my stamina, and my purpose, increase my faith. Is it possible . . . ?

All things are possible. So often faith comes through the fire of sorrow which purifies the soul as it destroys the self. Let faith build by recognizing My truth rather than by experience. Experience is not the best teacher. I am. Joyfully know that I knew you before I formed you in your mother's womb. I saw the days ahead, even this one. Do not be concerned for I have you in the palm of My hand. (Read Jeremiah 1:5.)

◇

Rest

And behold, a woman of Canaan came from that region and cried out to Him, saying, "Have mercy on me, O Lord, Son of David! My daughter is severely demon-possessed" (Matthew 15:22).

◆

Why is it so hard to rest and abide in You, Lord?

There are vexing spirits abounding in the world. But you are not at their mercy! Know that first. Also be aware that when you allow the little cares and frets to accumulate instead of bringing them to Me, you give a vexing spirit the space to land and stand. Cast down every thought that would cause you anxiety. Lose sight of all limitation and gain a new vision. Catch up to My schedule for your high calling. Abandon yourself to Me. I lay My right hand of blessing upon you. Receive ineffable strength and fearlessness to rest and abide. In My kingdom, rest is strength. (Read Ephesians 1:17–18.)

Comfort

**I will deliver you from the hand of the wicked,
and I will redeem you from the grip of
the terrible (Jeremiah 15:21).**

◆

*Lord, what is happening . . . ? The time draws
near.*

All that is happening to you is to bring
about an answer to your prayers. You have not
sought My help in vain. Know that your weariness and exhaustion are not signs of lack of
spirit. Tenderly I will see you through. And the
sunlight of My presence will bathe you on the
way. Trials, I promise, cannot do more than
work My will for you, and My will, you have
said, is your will. As you walk steadily forward,
I will guard your life. When you try feebly to
guard it yourself, you remove yourself from My
deliverance. Lean not to your own understanding and common sense. Trust Me with all your
heart . . . your moments . . . your life. That is
true commitment. (Read Psalm 25:10.)

August 27

◇

Protection

"No weapon formed against you shall prosper,
and every tongue which rises against you in
judgment you shall condemn. This is the
heritage of the servants of the LORD, and
their righteousness is from Me," says
the LORD (Isaiah 54:17).

◆

*This one thing I know: God is for me! I trust You
and Your promises, Lord, and stand on them. You
have already saved me from death and hell. Who else
could do such a thing! Let the enemy meet with his
hordes to perfect their plans against me or my family . . . and I will see My mighty Lord and King
dash them and their plans to the ground. Praise Your
promises!*

My child, no weapons fashioned against you
shall stand. I am greater than he that is in the
world! Hide under My almighty shadow and
My wings will protect you until the storm is
past. Oh, My love and faithfulness! My glory,
though high above the earth, is in you. (Read
Psalm 56:3 and 1 John 4:4.)

Fear and Faithfulness

Fear not, for I am with you; be not dismayed, for I am your God. I will strengthen you, yes, I will help you, I will uphold you with My righteous right hand (Isaiah 41:10).

♦

What is it, Lord? Speak, and I will listen.

Fear not! I will physically remove that place where Satan is attempting a stand. He will be utterly defeated. It is his last stand! You will be victorious. It will be his end . . . but for you, the beginning of a new life consecrated to My service, a life of power and joy and peace; a continual resting in Me will result, even when actively involved. As you go into the arena, I will be with you, holding your hand. I will protect your mind and emotions. My angels will be hovering about you, watching over every move. Know, envision My presence. Feel Me, see Me, hear Me. I will never leave you nor forsake you, My child. (Read Lamentations 3:22–23.)

August 29

◇

The God Who Heals

But those who wait on the LORD shall renew their strength; they shall mount up with wings like eagles, they shall run and not be weary, they shall walk and not faint (Isaiah 40:31).

♦

This morning I feel so quiet. I have nothing to say.

My beloved, you are right to keep silence. Renew your strength. Draw very near to Me. You are My beloved, whom I have chosen and grafted onto the tree of Abraham. Do not be afraid, for I will be with you as you go. I will steady those hands that touch you. I, the God who heals you, will keep you. I will strengthen you; yes, I will uphold you with My right hand. I say again: Fear not, I will help you. I am preparing you to be a new, sharp threshing instrument, having teeth, to help the poor and needy. I will open rivers in high places and fountains in the valleys, and will make the desert a pool of fertility. You will see it. (Read Psalm 46:10.)

A New Song

But now, thus says the LORD, who created you,
O Jacob, and He who formed you, O Israel:
"Fear not, for I have redeemed you; I have
called you by your name; you are
Mine" (Isaiah 43:1).

◆

Thank You, Father-God, for Your great love.

Bold new things do I declare! Before they
spring forth I tell you of them, that you may
sing unto Me a new song. Fear not. When you
pass through the waters, I will be with you, and
the rivers shall not overflow you; when you walk
through the fire, you will not be burned nor
scorched. You are My chosen witness. Know
that I am God. Do not dwell on former things,
dear one, neither consider the things of old, because I am going to do a new thing. I blot out
all transgressions. I will not remember your sins.
I will eradicate the decayed places and a new
foundation will be laid. You shall be built and
you shall be inhabited only by Me. You have
seen My glory! (Read Isaiah 43:1-5.)

August 31

◇

Salvation

But You, O LORD, are a shield for me, my glory and the One who lifts up my head (Psalm 3:3).

◆

Today I go, Lord, and I go in Your name. Keep my spirit pure in my suffering, for I know it is as nothing compared to the heart-hurting agony of body, mind, and spirit You suffered on the Cross. And when I return from the arena, I shall surely say of You: The Lord is all my righteousness, I stand secure in Him. Loving Lord, Thy will be done.

My child, you delight Me. Even to your old age, I am He who will lift up and carry, and even deliver you. I am God. There is none other like Me. Lift up your eyes and see the mighty army gathering in your defense; your enemies will be put far away from you, with no return passage. Yes, the things I have spoken to you I will bring to pass. My salvation will not tarry, for today has come. Be not afraid, for I am refining you, not with silver but with this furnace of affliction. And when it is over, you will come forth a polished shaft. (Read Isaiah 46:4.)

September

My soul, wait silently for God
alone, for my expectation
is from Him.

Psalm 62:5

September 1

◇

Strength

For the Lamb who is in the midst of the throne will shepherd them and lead them to living fountains of waters. And God will wipe away every tear from their eyes (Revelation 7:17).

♦

I have seen the mighty army that is on my side, Lord, and I am not afraid.

Did I not tell you ahead of time? Now awake and put on strength, for I have said the redeemed shall return with singing, and everlasting joy shall be upon their heads. You shall obtain gladness and joy, and sorrow and mourning shall flee away. Awake, awake, stand up, My beloved, put on strength, put on beautiful garments, for the unclean and the dead waste have been circumcised away. You are clean. You are Mine. (Read Isaiah 51:11.)

Healing

He is despised and rejected by men, a man of sorrows and acquainted with grief. And we hid, as it were, our faces from Him; He was despised, and we did not esteem Him (Isaiah 53:3).

•

Dear Jesus, You were despised and rejected. You carried our griefs and sorrows upon Your innocent, sinless body and mind. You were wounded for our transgressions and bruised for our iniquities. It is Your stripes by which we are healed. How can I ever thank You enough?

Love from a grateful heart and faith-filled spirit is quite enough. (Read Matthew 4:23–24.)

September 3

◇

Hearing and Obeying

Then the angel who talked with me answered
and said to me, "Do you not know what these
are?" And I said, "No, my lord." So he
answered and said to me: "This is the word
of the LORD to Zerubbabel: 'Not by might
nor by power, but by My Spirit,' says the
LORD of hosts" (Zechariah 4:5–6).

◆

*What art thou, O great mountain? Before the
Lord, you shall become a plain! Lord, I rest in quiet
expectancy, for I know that one blow struck at Your
right time is worth a thousand struck in my prema-
ture eagerness.*

My strikes are always on target. Never
wasted. But you must be ready to take My rod
in your hand when I say, or throw it down when
I say. This requires disciplined listening for My
command! It is not by might nor by power that
the mountain becomes a plain, but by My
Spirit. Rest. Watch. Wait. Until you blaze and
glow with love for My Son. And you will see
great and mighty things. (Read Zechariah 4:7.)

Encouragement

He has not dealt with us according to our sins,
nor punished us according to our iniquities. For
as the heavens are high above the earth, so great
is His mercy toward those who fear Him; as far
as the east is from the west, so far has He
removed our transgressions from us
(Psalm 103:10–12).

♦

*Lord, my heart bursts with songs of new life and
I bless myself with You, the God of Truth.*

The truth is that the former things are forgotten, not to be remembered nor come to
mind except for learning and blessing. Continue
your rejoicing, build your house, plant your
vineyard, for you shall long enjoy the work of
your hands. And because you trust, obey, and
glorify Me, it shall come to pass that before you
call I will answer, and while you are yet speaking, I will hear. I will extend peace like a river,
a mother's comfort to your hearts, and your
bones will flourish like an herb in springtime.
(Read Isaiah 65:24.)

Discipline

Delight yourself also in the LORD, and He shall give you the desires of your heart. Commit your way to the LORD, trust also in Him, and He shall bring it to pass. . . . Rest in the LORD, and wait patiently for Him; do not fret because of him who prospers in his way, because of the man who brings wicked schemes to pass (Psalm 37:4–5, 7).

♦

Because their hearts were tender and they humbled themselves before You, O God, You heard the cries of prophets and kings, great and small. O Lord, I want to observe the spirit of all the words of the Book of the Covenant and to obey every syllable spoken to my ear by the Holy Spirit. I know You are preparing me to speak Your Word, to write Your Words of blessing, encouragement, and exhortation.

And I will bring it to pass. As often as you must—a thousand times a day if necessary—bring your thoughts into captivity. Discipline your mind and emotions. Be patient and learn to wait with grace. (Read Proverbs 13:4 and 1 Peter 1:10.)

◇

Preparation

**For the vision is yet for an appointed time; but
at the end it will speak, and it will not lie.
Though it tarries, wait for it; because it will
surely come, it will not tarry (Habakkuk 2:3).**

◆

Almighty God, was I wrong about the vision?

Be patient! I will bring you out from under
the weights and pressures of unfinished projects
and difficulties. With vigor and changeless
power I will complete the tasks set before you
and make you sturdy and strong in faith. Ever
since the vision was given, I have been at work,
getting you into shape for the next phase . . .
but you keep trying to mold yourself into a
shape of your own ideal. Let Me put you on My
potter's wheel and whirl you as I like and, as
surely as I am God, the end will be ideal and
perfect. On time! But do not lose hope. You
must trust Me. I am the refiner and purifier and
finisher. Though the vision tarries, it will surely
come. Remember that the just live by faith.
(Read Proverbs 29:18 and Malachi 3:3.)

September 7

◇

Christ-Conscious

**And He [God] put all things under His [Jesus']
feet, and gave Him to be head over all things
to the church (Ephesians 1:22).**

◆

*Oh, Thou Christ of God, Head over all things,
unspeakable gift to us, help us to know in a new way
what it means to live in the enjoyment of our great
privileges, with an increasing passion to know You
better.*

Consciousness of Me and My love changes
all life. All life is made different. I give you
earthly friends, sweet and dear. But it sometimes
takes a crisis to reveal the great Friend who
stands by you. Make an effort to live up to our
noble friendship. Drink at My fountain. And let
new life spring forth. (Read Job 22:21.)

Restoration

For I know the thoughts that I think toward
you, says the LORD, thoughts of peace and
not of evil, to give you a future and
a hope (Jeremiah 29:11).

◆

*Great thanks unto Thee, O My God, that You
have rescued me and called me into rest and quiet.
Thank You, gracious Lord Jesus, for Your constant
intercession; my bruise was not incurable and my
wounds are not grievous. Thank You for all those who
pleaded my cause, for the pressing out and healing of
disease, for the doctor's skillful hands and astute
mind, for soothing medicines, and especially for the
angelic hosts You promised. Thank You for devouring
those who would have devoured me; and all that
would spoil, You have spoiled. Almighty Father, how
I praise You! Thank You for restoring my health.*

I will continue until I have healed all your
wounds and restored everything the canker-
worms have eaten. For I know the thoughts I
think toward you, My child, thoughts of peace
and restful understanding. (Read Psalm 107:7.)

September 9

◇

Sacrifice of Praise

Blessed is she who believed, for there will be a fulfillment of those things which were told her from the Lord (Luke 1:45).

◆

Lord, I believe all You have said to me.

And you shall have the abundance of peace and truth I promised. I am building you, as I have cleansed and pardoned you. Patience! Patience, My dear! Your voice will be filled with joy and gladness, and you shall be as the bride unable to be apart from the bridegroom—loving, adoring, praising Me for such great goodness, acknowledging My protection. The Lord is good, you will say, His mercy endureth forever. And you will be right. Continually bring your sacrifice of praise and I will perform that good thing I have promised. It is not a favor bought by praise, but the gracious way things are designed to operate. (Read Psalm 34:1.)

◇

New Ways to Praise

And those who know Your name will put their trust in You; for You, LORD, have not forsaken those who seek You (Psalm 9:10).

◆

You, O Lord, are the ecstasy and the reality. You keep my feet rooted soundly while You lift me upright and make my spirit soar. Practical. Quickening. Majestic. Holy. Abba.

I am Alpha and Omega, the totality of all things. Call upon Me. When you need protection I am a wall of fire; affection—the bridegroom; purpose—the Way, the Truth, and the Life; creativity—the Word of God. And for confidence, I am the lifter of your head. Find new ways of praising and worshiping, not for My magnification, but for your nourishment. Your private worship of Me is the single great essential for growth, character, and fitness. I am the same day after day after day. Enjoy Me. Be excited by My never-changing, ever-fresh provision. I am the hidden manna. (Read Zechariah 2:5; Psalm 3:3; Revelation 1:8.)

September 11

◇

Be Still

**Give unto the LORD the glory due to His name;
worship the LORD in the beauty of
holiness (Psalm 29:2).**

◆

*Look! How still they stand, the roses! Their
branches raised toward You, Lord, from whence com-
eth their life.*

And how firmly rooted they are. When the
strongest, coldest, or hottest winds assail them,
they flex even to the ground, yet they do not
break. Today they stand still and wait . . . wait
for a breath of air before they move. Look at the
beauty that waiting causes—the blooms, the
color, the dimension. And there, the dead,
dried-up flowers of another day, marring the
beauty, not just of itself but the entire garden.
No matter how the wind blows, the dead waste
tenaciously hangs on. It takes a decisive act, a
cut. A severing must be made. Prune back the
dead stuff. Look to the rose and learn. Learn to
be still and wait . . . and grow beautiful. (Read
Isaiah 61:1–3.)

Seek Me First

**And He Himself is the propitiation for our
sins, and not for ours only but also for
the whole world (1 John 2:2).**

◆

*Most holy Lord, our propitiation, thank You for
Your atoning sacrifice, which makes forgiveness possible. There is a cloud over my heart that keeps love
waiting in pain and tears for a healing to take place.
Lord, help me quick, to overcome.*

The first thing is to let go. Totally forgive.
And when the pain starts to go, be confident
that I will cause good to come. Have faith in
Me, not in the ministrations of others. I will
never fail you. And remember, whatever you
seek for yourself you must give up—things, circumstances, people. Do not make anything
more important, even for a moment, than Me.
I am all that is good and life-giving. And as you
seek and serve Me first, your whole body and
mind and spirit shall be filled with light. Oh,
My beloved, you are greatly blessed. (Read Matthew 6:14–15, 22 and 2 Corinthians 3:18.)

September 13

◇

My Secret Place

**But seek first the kingdom of God and His
righteousness, and all these things shall
be added to you (Matthew 6:33).**

♦

I forgive, Father. The hard part is not remembering.

I am your hidden manna, your stash. When
you look within and find nothing to sustain,
and nothing being offered by your friend, look
for Me in the secret place, My secret place. Take
the keys to the Kingdom, open the door, and
climb within; there you'll find all you need, all
provision. Fearless courage, full strength, comfort, freedom from hurt, creativity. I answer
your every appeal. Call the name, Jesus! And
watch circumstances and feelings change. When
others fail you or disappoint you, turn to Me!
Character is measured by your instant reactions.
Live up to My vision of you, through Christ. In
My secret place, you shall find rest. (Read Psalm
27:5.)

Depth of Prayer

**Blessed are the pure in heart, for they
shall see God (Matthew 5:8).**

◆

*It is not so simple, Lord, to enter into that trea-
sure chamber of the heart wherein the Kingdom of
God lies. Why does it take so great an effort and struggle to reach that state of prayer that is free from all
disturbance? Free me from analyzing and intellectu-
alizing, Father. Penetrate the marrow of my hu-
manness which limits so much of my relationship
with You to interesting words or fainthearted emotions. Give me spiritual eyes to see the truth of myself,
as well as Your truth.*

You are asking for a depth of prayer that chal-
lenges you to hide nothing from Me, absolutely
nothing. I see all, but only the pure in heart
shall "see" Me. (Read 1 John 5:14–15.)

September 15

◇

Security

The LORD is good, a stronghold in the day of trouble; and He knows those who trust in Him (Nahum 1:7).

♦

O Lord, You are altogether good and You have proven Yourself a stronghold in my day of trouble!

Though your enemies were many, still they were cut down. Hear Me when I say that though you were afflicted, you will be afflicted no more, nor will your affliction rise up a second time, for I have broken Satan's yoke, and burst your bonds asunder. Keep your fasts and vows, dear one, perform your feasts, take your trips, and continue in the abundant life, for the wicked one shall no more pass through you . . . he is utterly cut off. Continue to rest in Me. Be quiet. In that stillness your strength will come and be maintained. In returning and rest shall you be saved. In quietness and in confidence shall be your strength. (Read Nahum 1:8–15 and Isaiah 30:15.)

I Will Never Forsake You

**For he who has entered His rest has himself also
ceased from his works as God did from His
(Hebrews 4:10).**

◆

*Lord, You are larger than this sorrow that can
only be inflicted by one well loved. I forgive because I
must. You are the greatest example, my Christ, who
loved me through Your pain, and readily forgave. I
exalt You, Lord; Your mercy and lovingkindness led
me out of the bitter swamp and set my feet on solid
ground. There is no other like You.*

I am the Lord who heals you. Be calm and at
rest, anxious for nothing. When you cover your
plans with prayer, willing My will be done, then
I press forward, ahead of your reasoning, either
to change your attitude or the circumstance.
But beware of small, petty things with enor-
mous power to distract your attention from Me.
Be delivered from the passion to vindicate yourself. I did not defend Myself. I left all to the Father. You must do likewise. (Read Jeremiah
6:16; Exodus 15:26; Matthew 11:29.)

September 17

◇

My Secret Place

**Nevertheless when one turns to the Lord, the
veil is taken away (2 Corinthians 3:16).**

◆

*O Lord, how hidden my life was before I found
You. But my hiding place was never secure, for it was
necessary to make visits into the world. Even then, I
put a veil over my face so that no one would guess that
I was hidden. Had I removed the veil I would have
recognized the masks of friends behind which they,
too, were hiding.*

Yes, your mind was blindfolded. And many
remain until this day without the veil removed,
in pain and hopelessness. Transparency of heart
comes by the power of My Son, Jesus Christ.
My invitation is always extended, to live in the
secret place of the Most High, under the shade
of My almighty hand—a sure place within,
known only to Me . . . and Mine. When fear
and troubles come, be aware that you have ven-
tured out from under My covering. Run quickly
back to Me, your shelter and confidence. (Read
Proverbs 18:10; 29:25.)

Rest in My Secret Place

He who dwells in the secret place of the Most High shall abide under the shadow of the Almighty. I will say of the LORD, "He is my refuge and my fortress; My God, in Him I will trust" (Psalm 91:1-2).

♦

Lord, keep our eyes upon You as we take up our tasks. So much to do. . . .

In Me you live and move and have your being. My peace and joy I give, that you may be strong for the things you are to do on the front lines. But you must learn to rest your body, mind, and spirit. Learn to delegate responsibility. You are not to perform every needful task by yourself. Listen to My counsel. I am lightening your burden. As you rest in and rely on Me, things will be more easily accomplished. It is My re-creating power. Be not tempted to the point of view, "I must do it myself or it will not get done." I will do it, saith your Lord, as you dwell in My secret place, under My shadow. (Read Hebrews 3:15.)

September 19

◇

Encouragement

**These things I have spoken to you, that My joy
may remain in you, and that your joy
may be full (John 15:11).**

♦

*Lord Jesus Christ, help me to be a chariot of
fire . . . for You.*

You will be. I bear you up on wings to bring
you to Myself, aflame with My Spirit . . . that
your joy might be full . . . and others blessed.
(Read 1 Peter 1:7–8.)

◇

Silently Wait

Then Jesus answered and said to them, "Most
assuredly, I say to you, the Son can do nothing
of Himself, but what He sees the Father do;
for whatever He does, the Son also does
in like manner" (John 5:19).

◆

*Lord, strengthen us so that our lives express them-
selves as godly lives, not as human lives attempting to
be godly.*

They that *wait* upon Me shall renew their
strength. Be careful to *wait* on the Holy Spirit,
not creating thrills by your flesh, nor counter-
feiting My Spirit. Both result in spiritual destruction. Be quiet. Be still and *wait* for My
direction. Rest in Christ-thoughtfulness, not
self-thoughtfulness. Self prays for the awareness
of answered prayer instead of resting in the serene certainty that the Father is answering. That
rest cleanses the heart of improper motives and
attitudes. Silently *wait* for My supernatural solu-
tion. (Read Psalm 37:7–8.)

◇

Love

A new commandment I give to you, that you love one another; as I have loved you, that you also love one another (John 13:34).

◆

Heavenly Father, Your excellent majesty transcends every power which would tempt my tongue to gossip, criticize, or speak doubt. You have made me for Your pleasure, Lord, and I want to walk with You in the early morning light and hear You talk and get to know You. I would be presumptuous if You had not told me that You want to speak with me. Why, O Lord, You who love to make galaxies and totally mysterious things?

There is only one reason: I love you. When you allow that same love to take precedence in your life, you will be kept on the cutting edge of the front lines where I work. Let that same love and strength and beauty you have seen in Me touch an untouchable world through you. (Read Genesis 3:8.)

Trustworthiness

[Abraham,] who, contrary to hope, in hope believed, so that he became the father of many nations, according to what was spoken, "So shall your descendants be." He did not waver at the promise of God through unbelief, but was strengthened in faith, giving glory to God, and being fully convinced that what He had promised He was also able to perform (Romans 4:18, 20–21).

◆

Precious Father, God of truth, Truth itself, thank You for Your trustworthiness. You are risking more than we if Your promises are not kept. True, our souls are at stake, but You stand to lose Your character.

Nothing can possibly prevent Me from keeping and fulfilling My Word. My impeccable character guarantees it. I never make promises too good to be true. Let trustworthiness also be your aim . . . your promises honorable, your word absolute and unshaded. Put the sword of *pure love* to every prideful, unfaithful thing in your nature. (Read Titus 1:1–3.)

September 23

◇

My Presence Transforms

Now when He was asked by the Pharisees when the kingdom of God would come, He answered them and said, "The kingdom of God does not come with observation; nor will they say, 'See here!' or 'See there!' For indeed, the kingdom of God is within you" (Luke 17:20–21).

◆

The Kingdom of God is within me, O Lord. Jesus said it and I believe it! The Kingdom of God is at hand!

It is true. That is where you draw near to Me before you are conscious of My nearness. And promptly, lovingly I am there. For comfort or peace, confidence or companionship. Never lose heart or be wearied of turning . . . or forgetful. It is My presence that transforms all life from ugliness to beauty, from chaos to tranquillity, from hateful to loving, from disorder to harmony. (Read James 4:8.)

True Rest

I waited patiently for the LORD; and He inclined to me, and heard my cry (Psalm 40:1).

◆

Lord, it is so hard for me to slow down, inside and out.

As you are able to rest in the midst of celebration, chaos, or diverse situations, you will be able to accept the greatness of ministry, excellence of power, and assumption of responsibility that is in My plan for you. It will become easy, when you wait upon Me, to sense instinctively when you are off-center and hasten back into My presence. I will never fail to answer your call. Wait until My rest fills your soul. Rest that is fearless, calm, and immovable, free of want and ambition. True rest allows Me to flow through you unhindered, like a quiet stream, having but that one function and doing it well. When you learn this valuable lesson, you can do all things, for you will then be alert in a way barely glimpsed before. (Read Habakkuk 2:3.)

September 25

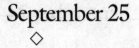

Rest

Come to Me, all you who labor and are heavy laden, and I will give you rest. Take My yoke upon you and learn from Me, for I am gentle and lowly in heart, and you will find rest for your souls. For My yoke is easy and My burden is light (Matthew 11:28–30).

◆

Lord, help us never to allow our relationship with You to become foggy, nor have the slightest trace of resentment pressed into our hearts or emotions over mistreatment or criticism.

There is only One who can accomplish it . . . Who made provision for your attitude to become the character of the Sermon on the Mount. It is simple and unstartling and spiritually upheaving. And one of the great lessons to learn: how to rest. How often must I repeat Myself? "Come to Me . . . and I will give you rest." Rest is a necessity—in returning and rest shall you be saved. In quietness is your strength. I will keep in perfect peace those whose minds are stayed on Me. (Read Jeremiah 6:16.)

Balance

Then I heard a loud voice saying in heaven,
"Now salvation, and strength, and the
kingdom of our God, and the power of His
Christ have come, for the accuser of our
brethren, who accused them before our
God day and night, has been cast
down" (Revelation 12:10).

◆

*I beseech You, Holy Spirit, help me to manifest
the same unsullied purity that was so prominent in
the life of Jesus.*

Just as you must confess and repent of all iniquities and sin, you must also see that morbid
sensitiveness does not rake up something for
your tender conscience to make much of. Jesus
allowed only the intense sensitiveness of My
Spirit to direct Him. Do likewise. The heroic
and balanced are always appropriate. (Read John
14:15–17.)

Obedience

Since you have purified your souls in obeying the truth through the Spirit in sincere love of the brethren, love one another fervently with a pure heart (1 Peter 1:22).

◆

Dear God and Savior, You are more than life, You are my eternal future. I focus my eyes on You. Take me under Your wing today.

You are as Aaron's plate of pure gold, like the engraving of a signet, on which is engraved: Holiness to the Lord. Wear the garment of praise, skillfully woven to set you apart, a special work to complete My body. Each of you is so much the same, yet so magnificently different—perfectly created for your particular role. All My longing is to give, to love. But I am not soft on anything that will ultimately ruin . . . see that you likewise do not sympathize with or be capricious toward sin. In your obedience, I shall be fully known. (Read Exodus 28:29.)

Speak the Truth

But I say to you, love your enemies, bless those who curse you, do good to those who hate you, and pray for those who spitefully use you and persecute you, that you may be sons of your Father in heaven; for He makes His sun rise on the evil and on the good, and sends rain on the just and on the unjust (Matthew 5:44–45).

◆

Some people who do not even know You seem to have more natural grace than some others who believe. Why, Lord?

I rain on the just and the unjust. When I speak, the words I say come to pass as surely as I spoke the world into being. Hear My voice. Do not allow the rationale of "I'm O.K., you're O.K.," to creep into your thinking or counsel. Speak repentance and turn away from idols. I have given everyone the ability to discern right from wrong. Be not deceived by "natural grace" but seek My incalculable wisdom. With love, speak the truth! Or do not speak at all. (Read Ezekiel 14:6–8 and Isaiah 9:7.)

September 29

◇

Desire Only My Will

For I am the LORD, I do not change; therefore you are not consumed, O sons of Jacob (Malachi 3:6).

◆

Radiant Lord Jesus, sun-ray of the Father's glory, shine in our hearts today and cause us to conform to Your image more and more.

When you look to Me for healing, strength, the dew of youth, power to face the future bravely, or the simple overcoming of fear, you shall know from personal experience that I am the Lord . . . with a gradual dawning or a sudden supernatural realization. And when you truly desire only My will, all the deep regions of your life that you have tried to change and longed to consecrate to Me will begin to harmonize. Simplify. Simplify your belief. (Read Psalm 116:6.)

Trust

**And I will pray the Father, and He will give
you another Helper, that He may abide with
you forever—the Spirit of truth, whom the
world cannot receive, because it neither sees
Him nor knows Him; but you know Him,
for He dwells with you and will be
in you (John 14:16–17).**

◆

*Word of God, Lord Jesus Christ, help us to live
worthy of Your high calling each day, each hour, each
moment.*

My Holy Spirit is the Helper. But you must
believe that My timing to plant, feed, water,
prune, pick, and squeeze the grape is perfect to
make the wine perfect. If you allow Me, you will
find that I produce the kind of bread, wine, and
fruit that is truly superior and produces after its
own kind. All I seek is your integrity of heart.
Transparent and honest with Me, you will recognize how true My character and promises are.
Ultimately, you will trust Me fully and love Me
with all your heart. (Read John 15:2.)

October

You will seek Me and find Me,
when you search for Me with
all your heart. I will be
found by you.

Jeremiah 29:13–14

October 1

◇

Change

**His heart is established; he will not be afraid,
until he sees his desire upon his enemies
(Psalm 112:8).**

♦

*In my dream I heard the words "Don't be afraid
to change." Lord, I know that You are always telling
us in Your Word, "Be not afraid; do not fear." And
in this You are specific. Lord, give me the grace and
poise and dignity with which to accept changes,
whether they be long range or immediate. Help me to
trust that You are in control of every change in my
life.*

As you rest in Me, you will destroy fear, gain
love, and be peaceful all the time. Change will
come as easily as rounding a turn in the road,
hardly considering, yet just knowing the way is
right. And your discernment will alert you to
any danger ahead. I will guide you. Be alert to
My touch, My voice. Trust Me. (Read Psalm
56:3.)

◇

The Blood of Jesus

**And being in agony, He prayed more earnestly.
Then His sweat became like great drops
of blood falling down to the
ground (Luke 22:44).**

◆

*O Lord, these crystal beads remind me
Of my sins so foul You bore,
Bloody red and tearful glistening,
You bought me and won the war.*

O My sweet and gentle servant,
    You were worth the pain and grief,
If you'd been earth's only sinner,
    I would still not sought relief.

(Read John 3:16.)

October 3

◇

Preparation

And whoever does not bear his cross and come after Me cannot be My disciple (Luke 14:27).

♦

Lord, never until this moment did I know (or have a notion) what was my cross to bear. When You said, "Whoever does not bear his cross and come after Me cannot be My disciple," I always wondered. Now, I see it has been my greatest aggravation . . . my great desire and my great burden all in one. And all along the way it has been a place to be broken, time and again. Only You know to what degree that is true. I carry my cross gladly, Father.

As you have said, only I know. And through it all, I have been preparing you. As you meet and commune with Me, I will show you what it is that you are being prepared for. I admonish you to pray without ceasing, commune with Me in your secret place, and rejoice always in the knowledge that I am God, and in Me is no darkness at all. Wait upon Me, and I will surely show you. (Read 1 Thessalonians 5:17–18; 1 John 4:4.)

◇

Work Done in Peace

**The work of righteousness will be peace, and
the effect of righteousness, quietness and
assurance forever (Isaiah 32:17).**

◆

*Lord, I pray for the ability to transmit ideas fully
formed and a point of view so well thought out that
it may be easily and articulately expressed. You have
called me to this task, O God; now sharpen my tools
that I may be a worthwhile servant where You have
placed me, and not appear the fool. Cleanse me, my
Father, of mind pollution, soulish alienation, and
disordered emotions, that I may freely communicate.*

Trust Me, My beloved, and be not afraid.
Would I allow you to play the fool? Just leave in
My hands the present and the future. I can
bring order out of chaos, good out of evil, peace
out of turmoil. Only believe! The success you
harvest will be the result of work done in peace.
Do not rush. Abide in Me and you shall bring
forth much fruit. (Read Exodus 4:10, 12; Isaiah
32:4.)

October 5

◇

Preparation

And He said, "My Presence will go with you, and I will give you rest" (Exodus 33:14).

♦

Lord, if Your presence does not go with me, I do not want to go . . .

I am present with you. With unveiled face, behold My glory and be transformed. Follow My Spirit's guidance to the wonderful illumination and fulfillment you seek; and waver not as you are being molded to fit the vision. I have not placed you in this place to break you, but to glorify Me. Do not despair, mourn, or complain as you approach the Promised Land, but believe that the climb up the mountain will bring you to your inheritance. Be fearless. Advance. Possess the land! And you will know such an outpouring of My fullness and power, earth-shaking answers to prayer, and intimacy of discipleship, that your past knowledge of Me will seem meager and paltry. Be not afraid, for My glory will go before you and behind you. (Read Exodus 33:13–20; Leviticus 9:6.)

Light

**And this is the condemnation, that the light
has come into the world, and men loved
darkness rather than light, because
their deeds were evil (John 3:19).**

◆

Great High Priest, King Jesus, while You represent us in the glory yonder, help us to practice the simplicity and leisureliness which should characterize Your children.

The disposition of sin is not all immorality and wrongdoing, but the propensity to be one's own god. I offer salvation from beginning to end. Do not refuse My offer. That is a critical moment when "light" is come. Only a disposition toward bustling about will keep you from the blessing of abiding, resting, trusting, and dwelling leisurely with Me. Relax. Be comfortable. Be disposed to humility. I teach not self-realization but perfection of character. As many as are led by My Father's Spirit are the sons and daughters of God and joint heirs with Me. (Read Hebrews 5:9; Romans 8:17.)

October 7

◇

Judgment

**Mark the blameless man, and observe the
upright; for the future of that man is
peace (Psalm 37:37).**

◆

Lord, I ask that the soul of this great leader, assassinated this morning, rest in peace; for You have said in Your Word that the end of the upright man is peace and that the peacemaker shall be called a child of God. Only You know and judge the heart of a man, but to me, he seemed a just and honest and upright maker of peace. Let it be so, Father.

My child, you have not gained godly wisdom to bear the knowledge or the burden of the Holy One. You can be sure that I will do right. Because I am just and righteous in all My judgments, the humble shall have the Kingdom of Heaven, those who hunger and thirst after Me shall be filled, the merciful shall obtain mercy, and the pure in heart shall see Me. (Read Matthew 5:3–9; Romans 2:11–15.)

◇

Rest of Spirit

Repent therefore and be converted, that your
sins may be blotted out, so that times of
refreshing may come from the presence
of the Lord (Acts 3:19).

♦

*O God, if we pine away because of our sins, how
can we then live in the "abundant life" You have
promised? More grace, O Lord, I cry for more grace!
Help me to live so as not to be scattered. I confess my
annoyance, my contending, my weakness, my unfor-
giveness—and I repent. Forgive me. Help me forgive
myself and stand patiently, trusting You when all else
has fallen beside me.*

When things pile up—responsibilities, pressure to perform, the busyness of appointments—then is the time to talk to Me. I know
the way seems hard, but as you rest in your
spirit, rejoicing in My presence, you will find
your body and mind being refreshed. (Read Isaiah 28:12; Ezekiel 33:4–5.)

October 9

◇

Filled Up with Me

Therefore He is also able to save to the uttermost those who come to God through Him, since He always lives to make intercession for them (Hebrews 7:25).

♦

Thank You, Lord, that You did not abandon us after You saved us. You sit in heaven still, ready to rid us of the leftover junk. O Jesus, how great Thou art! Give us that same loyalty to the Father that You have—singular and simple and faithfully honest.

Common sense and earthly intelligence are natural gifts to humanity, but supernatural sense is what contacts our Father. Take your eyes off your own unworthiness and fix them on My righteousness. Be naturally and supernaturally obedient, while allowing grace to bring you out of self-consciousness into God-consciousness. As you are filled up with Me, those fragments of junk will disintegrate and be no more. Trust Me. (Read Joshua 24:24; 1 Samuel 15:22.)

◇

Faith

**For we walk by faith, not by sight
(2 Corinthians 5:7).**

◆

*O Lord, give me expectant faith. Help me to see
Your books and magazines in the marketplace rather
than those which poison minds. Let them be living
candlesticks which attract and light up the spirits of
millions.*

Be not surprised, dear one, when your faith
turns to expectation, then to reality. Although
you do not yet see the results in the physical
world, it is already accomplished in the spiritual
dimension. And My timing is always perfect.
(Read 1 Chronicles 16:8–12.)

October 11

◇

You Are Being Changed

But we all, with unveiled face, beholding as in
a mirror the glory of the Lord, are being
transformed into the same image from
glory to glory, just as by the Spirit of
the Lord (2 Corinthians 3:18).

◆

*Just as the cloud images are so swiftly swept away
by the wind and other images are formed, that swiftly,
O God, do I want to be changed into the image of
Jesus. I want to shine with Your glory.*

Patience, My child; you are being changed.
As you provide the climate and prepare the
ground, I nourish the seed and cause it to grow.
The flowers, buds, and fruit follow as a natural
consequence, a law in operation. And when you
have a bumper crop, you will be the first to taste
the fruit. (Read Hosea 14:8.)

◇

Fear Is a Snare

**For God has not given us a spirit of fear, but
of power and of love and of a sound mind
(2 Timothy 1:7).**

◆

*O Lord, help me to serve You with a pure con-
science, casting down all fear. I know that Your gifts
are power, love, and sound-mindedness.*

The spirit of fear brings with it a characteristic which causes one to rise up in pride to defend
it or excuse it. Be not deceived! Fear of people
is a snare; fear of fear is a snare. Only godly awe
is freeing and liberating. Therefore, let Me persuade you to commit everything, every care, to
Me. Then hold fast, not by fleshly grit, but by
unfeigned faith, which comes by allowing My
Holy Spirit free access to your spirit. Break
through into a new, wide place. Trust Me. I
make everything work together for good for
those who love and trust Me. I have said it, and
it is so! (Read 2 Timothy 1:6–12; Romans
8:28.)

October 13

◇

Know My Word

Preach the word! Be ready in season and out of season. Convince, rebuke, exhort, with all longsuffering and teaching (2 Timothy 4:2).

◆

Lord, help us never to make a pretense of godliness but deny the power thereof; ever learning, yet never able to come to the knowledge of the truth. Make us bold to speak to those we feel might reject us, without fear of being scorned.

Dear one, you must not strive, but be gentle and patient with others and yourself, always loving as I have loved you, in humility instructing those who oppose. That is the way you awaken and recover those who have been taken alive by the enemy. Remember that My Word is profitable to live by, correct by, and reprove by. Know My Word! Be ready in season or out of season to do My work. I stand with you, strengthening you, delivering you, preserving you, putting the right words in your mouth. I trust you. Trust Me. (Read 2 Timothy 3:5–7, 16–17.)

◇

Release All to Me

**Whenever I am afraid, I will trust
in You (Psalm 56:3).**

◆

*O Lord, complete the good work You've begun in
our family as we have prayed and expectantly believed
since last Christmas; shine Your heavenly searchlight
into every dark and hidden corner of our personalities,
revealing what needs to be healed, delivered, corrected,
or disciplined. Thank You, dear Father, that we are
seeing the evidence of Your faithfulness. Continue,
complete us! Cause this Christmas to be a time of rejoicing, breakthrough, testimony, and freedom from
all the shackles of the past.*

Breakthrough comes as you release all to
Me . . . your mate, children, and friends. Expect
them to change. Release circumstances and the
need for your own way. Your release frees Me to
work in every situation. Praise Me in all things.
Know My Word. Fix your heart on Me. Awake
early and sing praises. I will deliver your soul
from death and deliver your feet from the snare
of the adversary. (Read Psalm 56:4, 13.)

October 15

◇

Preparation

For if you remain completely silent at this time, relief and deliverance will arise for the Jews from another place, but you and your father's house will perish. Yet who knows whether you have come to the kingdom for such a time as this? (Esther 4:14).

♦

Lord, help me to live in that secret place where there is always plenty, not poverty—where I know in my spirit that Your storehouse is overflowing and I have but to ask.

I have told you: You are a child of the King! The power to live in that secret place of refuge was yours even before you asked. Esther needed to have a call to come before the king. But My door is open to you all the time. All the training, teaching, cleansing, adorning has been for such a time as this, that you may not speak until it is time and that you may not hold your peace when it is time. (Read Psalm 51:10.)

◇

Disorder to Order

In God (I will praise His word), in the LORD
(I will praise His word), in God I have put
my trust; I will not be afraid. What can
man do to me? (Psalm 56:10–11).

♦

Thank You for Your presence, great creator of perfection, eliminator of every evil—every abnormal cell and maverick molecule in the body. Thank You for showing me how to war against the attackers of healthy cells and tissue, how to move mountains, or how to keep the ant hill from growing, using the mighty name of Jesus. Oh Lord, what power You share with us. Thank You for Your laws and principles which, like the law of gravity, are sure. I praise You for all that You know Yourself to be, Lord.

Praise is what changes disorder to order. Praise Me without ceasing. Be thankful and rejoice! Only turn your eyes on yourself when something is out of order. And in the name of My Son, Jesus, rout out all fear, disorder, chaos, abnormality, and depression. Then refocus your eyes on Me. (Read Colossians 2:5–7.)

October 17

◇

Guidance

Trust in the LORD with all your heart, and lean not on your own understanding; in all your ways acknowledge Him, and He shall direct your paths (Proverbs 3:5–6).

◆

Lord, thank You for the intimate connection we have with You... for Your care, for prayers answered, for healing and deliverance, all of which has given us a knowledge of You nothing can shake. But most of all, thank You for You.

Your feet are secure on the path as you acknowledge Me in all your ways. Trust Me with all your heart, for a new day is coming, a glad day, a season which cannot be compared to any other. The best news is: You are now ready to declare your love for Me in a unique way. You have not walked this way before. Be not anxious. Simply stay far enough behind My lead to get a proper perspective of where I am going. It will save you time. Walk softly. And don't forget to watch. (Read Isaiah 30:21.)

◇

Humility

I am the vine, you are the branches. He who abides in Me, and I in him, bears much fruit; for without Me you can do nothing (John 15:5).

◆

Dear Jesus, there are many in the world who would die for a good cause, but You died for us though we were a lost cause. How great You are! Oh, how I yearn to love You more . . . with divine love; let it flow from Your throne through me, back to You!

What you ask is easy . . . all it takes is yielding to My holy disposition. Thinking that you are either a somebody or a nobody will lead to discouragement, which is disillusioned self-love. Concentrate your soul on My nature and character. You can do it. Your failures have taught you humility, and your success has taught you to keep your eyes on Me, without whom you can do nothing. It is not a threat, just a simple truth. (Read Luke 1:37.)

October 19

◇

Surrender All

Come to Me, all you who labor and are heavy laden, and I will give you rest (Matthew 11:28).

◆

Lord, help me to make the distinction between Your will and mine in all things. . . .

It is inexcusable folly to try to please Me your own way. Every believer must recognize the importance of being entirely surrendered to My will: nothing more, nothing less, nothing else. Surrender costs, but in the end reaps rich rewards. Self-consciousness is the first thing that upsets and interrupts completeness in Me, for if it is allowed, by slow degrees it will awaken self-pity, which is from the pit of hell. Stop turning and toiling, disputing, defending, and blaming. It is an urgent warning! Renounce self and you shall be a vessel of honor, ready for My use. I love you, and offer you freedom from yourself. And rest. The rest that replaces and restores. Your choice. My grace. (Read Matthew 11:29–30; Luke 11:2; 2 Timothy 2:21.)

Endless Love

Now before the feast of the Passover, when Jesus knew that His hour had come that He should depart from this world to the Father, having loved His own who were in the world, He loved them to the end (John 13:1).

♦

O Lord, give me power to excel in all things You require of me.

My love is the greatest power, the strongest force in creation. If you have love, you have the very essence of My power. The cry for more love is always heard and answered. Even now, I pour out My divine love upon you, to you, through you to others. Love Me first, then others, then yourself . . . all require a dying to your own way, your own interests, a lowering of your own defenses. Acknowledge that which is hidden. Be unpitying with yourself that you may respect yourself, that you may grow to love yourself as I know and love you. Only then can you love your neighbor as yourself. (Read John 13:8–9, 34.)

October 21

◇

Trust

Therefore whoever humbles himself as this little child is the greatest in the kingdom of heaven (Matthew 18:4).

◆

Lord, I yearn for that unaffected loveliness which is characteristic of You and unaware of itself.

Impulse and temperament only hinder your development. Self-conscious small-mindedness, defensive grumbling, and impetuous pride cannot stand a crisis or the stress of everyday drudgery. Be content never to do anything exceptional for Me; simply allow Me to use you as I see fit. My supernatural grace breeds in you those attributes which you need. When you trust Me and leave everything to Me, you shall be unaffected and lovely. (Read 2 Corinthians 12:9.)

October 22

◇

Praise and Thanksgiving

You are my hiding place; You shall preserve me from trouble; You shall surround me with songs of deliverance (Psalm 32:7).

♦

Lord, sometimes I feel as if time is dwindling away: the morning is soon gone, the afternoon light fades, the night is upon us, and so much is left undone. I want to rest in You as You have directed, yet I feel tyrannized by the hour of the day. Please hear me, O God; deliver me from this self-reproach and bless me according to Your tender mercies.

The only day that is wasted is one in which you have not praised Me with a song or magnified Me with thanksgiving, not because I am hungry for it, but because your soul (your mind and emotions) will starve without it. From that beginning, your day is off to the right start. Then you are ready to drink up the hours with confidence, bowing your self-interest before Me, the God of Love who is not easily moved or provoked. (Read Ephesians 5:19–20.)

October 23

◇

Trust

I love those who love me, and those who seek
me diligently will find me (Proverbs 8:17).

♦

*Early in the morning I rise up to greet You, Lord,
to watch with You. I seek more of You today . . .
stronger ability to perceive Your great worth, a mind
to remember and recall Your Word, concentration
that does not have to contend or compete, and a voice
to proclaim Your prophecy simply. It's a lot to ask, but
I know that You hold the answers to all that I am
and ever will be and ever need to be.*

I am the Lord thy God, who brought you
out of the land of Egypt. The longer you live
with Me, the more like Me you will grow. Just
as a child seeks to imitate its mother and father,
your abilities, mind, and concentration seek the
nourishment of My wisdom and perception.
Strive not in the matter. Simply trust Me, for I
will bring it to pass. Rely on Me alone. Look for
no other help. Trust not in words because they
are already formed, but trust in My Word. (Read
1 Corinthians 14:1.)

Repentance

But we have renounced the hidden things of shame, not walking in craftiness nor handling the word of God deceitfully, but by manifestation of the truth commending ourselves to every man's conscience in the sight of God (2 Corinthians 4:2).

♦

I renounce the spirits of manipulation, preachiness, wanting my own way, criticism, and judgment, which link hands with one another to deceive me, destroy fruitfulness, and shrink the joy and satisfaction of living. I renounce them in Your mighty name, Jesus, the name which has power to bind and loose.

You have renounced and you are free. It is when you see sin and do not confess and part with it that the spirit of confusion enters. Prayer penetrates that spiritual fog. If you see yourself using excuses, blaming others or circumstances for your situation, it is a sign pointing you to repentance. The truth is an excellent starting place in seeking the answer to any dilemma. Repent quickly and be free. (Read Acts 17:26–31.)

October 25

◇

Choose Freedom

I will give you the keys of the kingdom of heaven, and whatever you bind on earth will be bound in heaven, and whatever you loose on earth will be loosed in heaven (Matthew 16:19).

◆

Thank You, Lord, for putting us through the seasons of growth—for bending, breaking, and molding us. Don't stop until You are pleased to say: This is My man, this is My woman in whom I am well pleased. And then don't stop, Lord, throughout eternity.

Remember always, I have chosen you! I have given you the keys of My Kingdom. I adjure you to take the key to that room you have kept locked for fear others would see it . . . and unlock it. Then you will be free. The fear may be worse than what you find in the room. Do not be afraid to expose it, to look at it. Do not wear those grave clothes any longer. Be free. (Read Ephesians 1:4.)

Be Not Deceived

Then the people of the land tried to discourage
the people of Judah. They troubled them in
building, and hired counselors against them to
frustrate their purpose all the days of Cyrus
king of Persia, even until the reign of
Darius king of Persia (Ezra 4:4–5).

◆

*O Father, strengthen our weak knees and build
us up. Let this be the day when we experience a breakthrough. Put words in our mouths—words of wisdom,
humility, reality, and love—and cause us to speak
with all calmness and dignity.*

The foundation of your temple has been
laid. Do not be afraid to face anyone, for I have
made you strong. Watch out for your adversary!
Beware of those who would say: Let us build
with you, for we seek your God as you do. Be
not deceived, but be discerning. What are their
fruits? Will they weaken your strong hands?
Trouble you in the building? Hire counselors
against you to frustrate your purpose? Ask for
all wisdom. (Read James 1:5; Proverbs 4:7–13.)

October 27

◇

Security

Then the children of Israel, the priests and the Levites and the rest of the descendants of the captivity, celebrated the dedication of this house of God with joy (Ezra 6:16).

•

Lord, will I never be satisfied with what You have already done in me? Will I never stop complaining and bothering You for ever deeper, ever greater growth?

Your foundations are firm and secure, My child. But you are challenged by the building you see as yet unfinished. That is no sin unless you become discouraged by things undone, by being torn down and rebuilt, or by having additions to the original plans. Welcome change! For one day, you will look about and see the building is complete. But even then, all is not finished; then comes the furnishing. I have prepared great spaces where you will be replenished, as well as places of feasting and rejoicing. Rejoice now in hope, and you will not be ashamed later when there is evidence to rejoice about. (Read 2 Corinthians 13:9.)

◇

Love

I am my beloved's, and his desire is toward me (Song of Solomon 7:10).

◆

To know You is to love You, Lord.

And you, My beloved. (Read Song of Solomon 2:4.)

Security

Because you have made the LORD, who is my refuge, even the Most High, your dwelling place, no evil shall befall you, nor shall any plague come near your dwelling; for He shall give His angels charge over you, to keep you in all your ways. In their hands they shall bear you up, lest you dash your foot against a stone (Psalm 91:9–12).

◆

Lord, bless me always to be the maker of joyful sounds. Teach me to number my days, not wasting one, that I might apply my heart to wisdom, and let Your beauty be upon me.

As you dwell with Me you will reflect My beauty, until people look at you but see Me. My angels are dispatched to take charge of you, deliver you, and honor you. I have a long life planned for you, because you have made Me your habitation. (Read Psalm 91.)

Wait

For thus says the Lord GOD, the Holy One of Israel: "In returning and rest you shall be saved; in quietness and confidence shall be your strength." But you would not (Isaiah 30:15).

♦

Lord, how difficult it is to wait. Show me how to rest in You in the midst of undone things. Help me to say sincerely, "Thy will, Thy timing be done and not my own."

It is one of the last and hardest lessons to learn . . . waiting. But once learned it will revolutionize your walk with Me. (Read Isaiah 30:18; 40:31; 2 Thessalonians 3:5.)

October 31

◇

Wait

For since the beginning of the world men have not heard nor perceived by the ear, nor has the eye seen any God besides You, who acts for the one who waits for Him (Isaiah 64:4).

♦

Lord, at the end of every inning, I think I have learned the art of waiting . . . but this is a new place. Only by Your grace does waiting not become empty and hopeless.

"The vision is yet for an appointed time; but at the end it will speak, and it will not lie. Though it tarries, wait for it; because it will surely come." Wait, and believe! I waited *patiently* in the day of Noah while the ark was being prepared—so that eight souls might be saved. As you wait, other people and other circumstances are being readied, so that all things may work together for the greatest result. Oh, My beloved, what I have prepared for those who wait upon Me! They will never be penalized. (Read Habakkuk 2:3.)

November

. . . to hear all the things
commanded you by God.

Acts 10:33

November 1

◇

Joy

Then he said to them, "Go your way, eat the
fat, drink the sweet, and send portions to those
for whom nothing is prepared; for this day is
holy to our LORD. Do not sorrow, for the
joy of the LORD is your strength"
(Nehemiah 8:10).

◆

*Dear Lord, cause me to overflow with joy—that
floods my being with love, that disallows soulish and
physical happenings to get me down; that makes
sounds You love, joyful noises that keep my spirit soaring toward You. And let it be contagious to my family
and everyone I meet.*

In My presence is fullness of joy. (Read
Psalm 16:11.)

◇

Prophecy

**And you, son of man, prophesy to the
mountains of Israel, and say, "O mountains
of Israel, hear the word of the LORD!"
(Ezekiel 36:1).**

◆

*Heavenly Father, I thank You for Your words to
me last night: "I will settle you after your old estates
and will do better for you than at your beginnings,
and you shall know that I am the Lord."*

Yes, My child, now you have the mind of
Christ. Use it. You have been praying for My gift
of prophecy. Use it. Speak these words to My
church: "You will not have to fight in this battle, for the zeal of the Lord of Hosts shall perform it. But there is something I require of you,
saith the Lord. Take your eyes off your feet and
walk upright. I say to all of you: I am the Way.
I am the Light. And I will lead you out into the
glorious sunlight of My presence, where you
can be purified by praise and thanksgiving, and
be a joyful sound in My ear." (Read Joel 2:28;
1 Corinthians 14:5.)

November 3

◇

Redemption

Therefore, as through one man's offense judgment came to all men, resulting in condemnation, even so through one Man's righteous act the free gift came to all men, resulting in justification of life (Romans 5:18).

♦

Lord, strengthen my faith. It is difficult for me to "glory in tribulation" that the virtue of patience be produced. O God, what is the answer?

You are not saved by believing; you are saved when you realize what I have done for you through My Son's death . . . and believe it. The same with patience or any other facet of redemption. Repentance does not do it. Repentance is only the sign that you know what Christ has done. But when you turn, trust, and obey, instantly My Son's atonement covers you supernaturally, just as if you had bought it yourself. This single truth cannot be known by human logic, for it is a miracle. The only way to "glory in tribulation" that produces patience is in *knowing* this truth. (Read Romans 5:3.)

◇

No Other Gods

He will not be afraid of evil tidings; his heart is steadfast, trusting in the LORD (Psalm 112:7).

♦

My heart is fixed, O God. I wake early to visit and watch with You. Be Thou exalted in Your great holiness. Through You I shall do valiantly. For You tread down all the enemy's troops before me.

Because your heart is fixed, you shall not be afraid. Fear of Me is the beginning of wisdom . . . and a good understanding comes to those obedient to My commands. Trust Me, ever more and more, for I raise the poor from the dust and set them with princes and presidents. Let your heart never be swayed by idols. Build no gods . . . self, money, fame, for they are unfeeling and indifferent. Man makes gods like himself but they are far beneath him. Thus when man becomes like his god, he becomes less than himself . . . unfeeling and indifferent. But those whose God I am are being changed into My likeness, becoming infinitely more than themselves. (Read Psalm 115:4–8.)

November 5

◇

Provision

It is the Spirit who gives life; the flesh profits nothing. The words that I speak to you are spirit, and they are life (John 6:63).

♦

Lord, You have blessed us with abundant life, while some of our friends suffer great lack, physically and financially.

My Holy Spirit hungers to bless them. I stand ready for My glory to fill their lives as it fills yours, and give them peace and freedom from fear. Rest easy, My child, for I am stirring their spirits. In lack, their souls may be saved. Let the love and abundant life and resources that I have given you be used, the teaching passed on . . . for I will replenish and give you more. (Read Psalm 107:9.)

Guidance

A good man deals graciously and lends; he will guide his affairs with discretion (Psalm 112:5).

♦

Help me, O Lord, to guide my affairs with grace, discretion, righteousness, and fullness of compassion.

You will deal wisely because I have taught you My statutes. Do not be suspicious, but do not put your confidence in man. It is I who hear all of your distress signals, and I hold the answer to every problem. (Read James 3:17.)

November 7

◇

Blessed Are They

At midnight I will rise to give thanks to You, because of Your righteous judgments (Psalm 119:62).

♦

This is the day the Lord has made. We will rejoice and be glad in it!

Blessed are: the sincere who are constantly adjusting . . . those who cleanse themselves by taking heed to My Word . . . those who learn My principles and meditate upon Me . . . those who keep their eyes open to the wondrous things I am doing . . . those who choose the way of truth and wholeheartedly observe it . . . those who walk in liberty and are not ashamed to speak My Truth. Blessed are those who sing songs of praise and rise in the night to watch and give thanks, for their hearts shall be healthy, their minds sound, their power great, and their habitation safe. (Read Psalm 118:24; 119:105.)

◇

Love

For God so loved the world that He gave His only begotten Son, that whoever believes in Him should not perish but have everlasting life (John 3:16).

◆

Holy, undefiled Savior, You became us, took our awful sins upon Yourself, and died for us. O what love, O what wondrous love, O what a love is this!

Now that you have witnessed My all-giving, thoroughly selfless love, you must attempt to emulate it. I dearly love you. (Read Deuteronomy 6:5.)

November 9

◇

Holiness

Beloved, now we are children of God; and it
has not yet been revealed what we shall be, but
we know that when He is revealed, we shall be
like Him, for we shall see Him as He is. And
everyone who has this hope in Him purifies
himself, just as He is pure (1 John 3:2–3).

◆

*Dear Lord Jesus, You have called us to be like
You, so that when You appear we may have confidence
and not be ashamed.*

When I come, you will be like Me, for you
shall see Me as I am. And everyone who has this
hope should purify himself, even as I am pure.
This admonition is not meant as a burden but as
a blessing. Do not fear that you can never attain
holiness. That fear—that which would keep you
from attempting the deepest, most godly walk
because you might fail—is a lie of the enemy,
who will do anything to keep you from growing. Start where you are, with the tiniest step.
You will see. I am here to meet you where you
are. Begin! (Read Hebrews 12:10–11.)

◇

Holiness

**My soul waits for the Lord more than those
who watch for the morning—yes, more
than those who watch for the
morning (Psalm 130:6).**

◆

*I wait for You, O Lord; my soul does wait. And
in Your Word do I hope. I study to make myself approved, but only You can anoint my words.*

Beloved, teach out of your own experience,
what I am teaching you: a deeper level of repentance, understanding, forgiveness, holiness. Tell
them that men are the head, the ruler in the
home, but that women are the heart and have
a greater influence on the sons and daughters of
tomorrow, for good or evil. Remind them that
I return goodness to those who expect goodness
from My hand. As they believe, it shall be done.
I make wellness of the soul in the family, the
home, the community, the nation. My blessing
makes one rich and adds no sorrow to it. Expect
it. (Read Lamentations 3:25; Proverbs 10:22.)

November 11

◇

Vulnerable Heart

**Sing, O daughter of Zion! Shout, O Israel!
Be glad and rejoice with all your heart,
O daughter of Jerusalem! (Zephaniah 3:14).**

◆

*You have extended Your blessing to me far beyond
all I could ever hope or imagine, Lord, and I shout
aloud for joy!*

And I will continue to bless you as you open
your heart in obedience. I will perfect that
which concerns you. I will never leave you nor
forsake you. You are My beloved and I am
yours. Though you walk in the midst of trouble
I will revive you. You shall be a lover and help-
meet to your mate, an influence of great value
to your children and to your children's children.
(Read Philippians 1:6.)

Silence

Words of the wise, spoken quietly, should be heard rather than the shout of a ruler of fools (Ecclesiastes 9:17).

•

Silence is a fearful thing, creating an uncomfortable nervousness in our society. We fear it is an empty, gaping vacuum which will swallow us up. Help us, Lord, to accept the quiet as full and rich, immeasurably divine and sacred.

What a power your word would have if you could gently and carefully learn to convert that empty, anxious restlessness into a full and serene silence. Let your behavior and your word enable others to befriend Me in silence. (Read 1 Peter 3:4.)

November 13

◇

The Easy Way

And the LORD said, "My Spirit shall not strive
with man forever, for he is indeed flesh; yet
his days shall be one hundred and twenty
years" (Genesis 6:3).

♦

*Lord, is it wrong of me to want an easy life, not
wanting to wrap my arms around sorrow and suffering but to embrace joy and peace and what is lovely?
To pray for ease in fasting? Is it lazy to pray for a
quick obedience so that I will not have to suffer?*

O My child, life is not easy because man has
distorted all that I meant it to be. What was a
straight path has been made into a way of de-
viousness and evil, filled with stones of difficulty. But My children do not have to walk that
way, for I have made possible a new and living
way of the Spirit. How you react to obstructions
in your path determines the ease, grace, and
poise with which you walk. As you accept My
principles of conduct, I show you the
step-by-step method of life. (Read Genesis 6:5,
11; John 16:33; Hebrews 10:20–22.)

Holiness

**But as He who called you is holy, you also be
holy in all your conduct, because it is written,
"Be holy, for I am holy" (1 Peter 1:15–16).**

◆

*Thank You, Lord, for making my mind even bet-
ter—filled with remembrance and order—and I know
it all comes from You. Thank You for those who pray
for us. O Lord, is there anything more wonderful
than being used by You? No, Lord, nothing!*

You are precious, My child. Your obedience
is pleasant to Me. Continue to live in the message that I give you today. . . . Be holy as I am
holy—complete and whole, lacking nothing.
Run from evil and be filled up with Me. (Read
Psalm 86:11–12.)

◇

Diligence

For the perverse person is an abomination to the LORD, but His secret counsel is with the upright (Proverbs 3:32).

◆

Lord, Thou hast done great things in this place . . . in me. Help us to follow hard after You, and walk softly before You.

Lean your ear close to My throne and I will whisper the secrets of My Kingdom. Stay much in My Word and study to make yourself approved. I reward those who seek Me diligently, and they will find Me who search for Me with all their hearts. Let your heart not stray away in flights of fancy but keep it stayed on Me, basking in My sunlight, walking and talking with Me in the early morning and the cool of the evening. Your faith pleases Me. You are precious in My sight. Your obedience blesses My heart. Know My character and you cannot help but grow like Me. To know Me is to love Me, for I am love. (Read Hebrews 11:6.)

November 16

◇

Peace and Plenty

Depart from evil and do good; seek peace and pursue it (Psalm 34:14).

♦

Dear Lord, give us Your Word this morning for our friends, for it seems as if they cannot hear Your voice.

Envision peace, pursue it, and pray for it. Only in My peace shall you, or they, have peace. Let not your prophets and profiteers deceive you; neither hearken to your own dreams which *you* cause yourself to dream, for they can also prophesy falsely. Those who wait upon the flesh shall perish after the flesh. I say wait . . . wait upon Me, and I will visit you and give you My good Word, which none can gainsay. I will also perform it, and not you yourself. For I know the thoughts I think toward you, thoughts of peace and not of evil to give you an expected end. But you must call and come and seek and pray! Those who wait upon Me will not be penalized, but will reap great rewards of peace and plenty. (Read Jeremiah 29:11–12.)

November 17

◇

Divine Care

O LORD, You have searched me and known me.
You know my sitting down and my rising
up; You understand my thought afar
off (Psalm 139:1–2).

◆

*Thank You, Father God, for the fire we've been
through, the refining process, the trying. But most of
all, for answering when we call upon You. You alone
are God, our God, almighty and wonderful!*

And you are My children. I will perfect that
which concerns you. I have searched you and
know you. I know your days and understand
your thought. I am acquainted with all your
ways; there is not a word in your tongue that I
am not altogether familiar with. How could you
flee from My presence, and where would you go
without My Spirit? Even in your mother's
womb I covered you. You are fearfully and won-
derfully made. I even chose your hands, your
eyes and mouth, when as yet you did not exist.
Yes, I know how to take care of you. (Read Jeremiah 1:4–5.)

◇

Be Not Shaken

Even there Your hand shall lead me, and Your right hand shall hold me (Psalm 139:10).

♦

Precious Father, I need an encouraging word today.

I say to you: Be not shaken in your mind, nor troubled, neither by spirit nor by word. Let no one oppose or deceive you. I, the Lord, shall consume wickedness with the spirit of My mouth. Stand fast. Hold the principles you have been taught. You are established for such a time as this. Go forth, and let your prayer and song of praise go before you, for I have set a watch upon your mouth, and I keep the door of your lips. Trust Me. Wait for the answers. Do not be rushed or pressed. You have the answers, for I have taught you well! (Read 1 Chronicles 16:9.)

November 19

◇

Guidance

**But the Lord is faithful, who will establish you
and guard you from the evil one
(2 Thessalonians 3:3).**

◆

*Lord, I thank You for Your grand provision. Let
us not waste the talents and gifts You have given us,
but pay careful attention to the guiding of Your Holy
Spirit. We do not want to go anywhere without You,
Lord, and if You go not with us, what good is there
in going?*

I shall keep you from all evil. But you must
rule your own spirit. Direct your heart into love
of Me. And withdraw yourself often into that
silent place of communion with Me. I am your
all-sufficient One. (Read Proverbs 16:32.)

◇

Source of All Wisdom

"But the word of the LORD endures forever."
Now this is the word which by the gospel
was preached to you (1 Peter 1:25).

◆

Lord, why is it that we experience so much of Your
grace and some others have such a struggle?

Most of My critics have never read My
Word, nor given a thought to seeking the truth
of it. Because you know My character and My
ways, the answers you need on earth will come.
When you see Me face to face, through truly
spiritual eyes, you will not find the need to in-
quire of anything. In that moment all your
questions will be totally satisfied, for I am the
answer to all things. Grace and peace are
multiplied to you through knowledge of Me
and of My Son, Jesus, whom I suspended in
time on the earth, to show you what I, the Divine Father, am like. Stay with Me and I will give
you all things pertaining to life and godliness.
You are attached to the source of all wisdom.
(Read 1 Peter 1:3–9; 1 Corinthians 13:12.)

November 21

◇

Paralyzing Analyzing

**Immediately there fell from his eyes something
like scales, and he received his sight at once;
and he arose and was baptized (Acts 9:18).**

♦

*Dear Lord, forgive me for being less than what
You've made me to be. Forgive the pride that would
rather be some image I have of myself. I renounce the
need to impress, the need to be approved of. O my God,
Thou art great and powerful in the pulling down of
strongholds. I confess my lack, and I throw myself on
Your mercy. Make my eye single toward You, Lord,
and grant me a calm heart and presence of mind.*

Your paralyzing and unfruitful way of analyzing yourself is coming to an end. You are already sensing the taste of what is to come . . .
when fear will no longer diminish your perception. Don't hide from Me! Listen to My whisper when I tell you to separate yourself from the
crowd. Listen when I whisper, for I will not
shout above the din. With My friends, shouting
should not be necessary. (Read Acts 9:1–22.)

Love

**But whoever keeps His word, truly the love of
God is perfected in him. By this we know
that we are in Him (1 John 2:5).**

♦

I just want to rest on Your lap this morning, Father. Looking into Your face, I am perfectly at peace. Why is it so hard for me to do what You have whispered to me to do?

Remember, beloved, even if you speak with the tongue of an angelic being, if you do not extend My love, you are as one beating on an off-key piano. Only what is done in My love lasts. The fame of the world, the applause for one who compels admiration, is all worthless if it is without My supernatural quality of love. I have ordained that you be a simple and fruitful carrier of My Word. Do not try to be what you are not. You are a lovely woman of God, and I will supply you with all you need, when you need it. *Forget about yourself,* so shall you bear much fruit. (Read 1 John 4:7; Psalm 81:10.)

November 23

◇

Power

Jesus Christ is the same yesterday, today, and forever (Hebrews 13:8).

●

Lord, teach us more of what You are like.

I gave you Jesus that you might see what I am like. Only man limits the powerful and miraculous things I want to do today on earth. I am a God of resurrection and life. See that! I restore and redeem and break through the darkness. I am the same yesterday, today, and forever. (Read John 10:27–30.)

Holiness

**But as He who called you is holy, you also be
holy in all your conduct, because it is written,
"Be holy, for I am holy" (1 Peter 1:15–16).**

♦

*Lord, help us to be leaders in loving, leaders in
forgiveness and reconciliation, leaders in right communication, letting our word be yes for yes and no for
no.*

Words beyond or falling short of those
which are honest come of evil and not of good.
I am calling you to be perfect, holy as I am holy.
You are responsible and accountable for all you
know. Do nothing to be applauded by men and
women: neither giving, praying, or fasting. Listen to Me, for I will guide you. Draw away into
the secret place of My Kingdom within you,
even as you speak with those to whom I send
you. There you will be dwelling with Me, waiting for the right words at the right time. Learn
a different, deeper level of communicating with
Me, in the presence of those who do not believe. (Read Matthew 5:44–46.)

November 25

◇

Light

**If we say that we have fellowship with Him,
and walk in darkness, we lie and do not
practice the truth (1 John 1:6).**

◆

*Make an obedient spirit to flourish in us and in
all our family, Lord.*

The light of the body is the eye: If your eye
is single toward Me, your whole body shall be
full of light. If your light is extinguished, the
darkness is even greater because of its potential
for good. And if your eye is evil, your body shall
be full of darkness. You must choose to serve Me
or the world, not just at the beginning when
you are born of My Spirit, but at each juncture,
each stretching point. Guard your thoughts,
that your eye remain single . . . take no thought
of how you appear to others, and be not anxious
about what you eat, drink, or wear. I am your
provider. I know what you need. As you seek
My Kingdom first, singly, choosing My right-
mindedness, all these other things shall be
yours. (Read Matthew 6:22–23, 33.)

Beauty of Character

**For bodily exercise profits a little, but godliness
is profitable for all things, having promise of
the life that now is and of that which is
to come (1 Timothy 4:8).**

◆

*Dear Father, I see the lines forming what will be
tomorrow's wrinkles; and I see my beauty fading, my
body losing the elasticity and fast-responding muscle
tone it has always had. Help me to know how to react
with dignity and poise and grace to what I see.*

My Son was not housed in a body so beautiful that He would be followed and adored for
His physical appeal. He was to the eye of the
world One to be despised. But to discerning
ones, the Spirit housed in that body was so
beautiful as to lack nothing. As your outer
beauty diminishes, pray for faith to see the
beauty of My character being worked in your
spirit. I love you as you are. I loved you even
before you were lovable. (Read Isaiah 53:2.)

◇

Balance

Judge not, that you be not judged. For with
what judgment you judge, you will be judged;
and with the measure you use, it will be
measured back to you. . . . Hypocrite! First
remove the plank from your own eye, and then
you will see clearly to remove the speck from
your brother's eye (Matthew 7:1–2, 5).

◆

*Lord Jesus, I pray for the right balance between
discernment and judgment, that I not be a hypocrite,
entertaining some sin in my own life that I would
rebuke and despise in another. Help me first to have
the discipline, courage, and right-mindedness to correct myself before I go to my family or friends with a
procedure to get rid of what I see in them.*

Your prayer is heard, My child. You have requested the very thing that allows you to see
clearly the mote in the eye of another. And
when you counsel, counsel as you would be
counseled, even in the same spirit, with understanding and patience, and above all, love.
(Read Romans 14:12–13, 19.)

Be Cleansed

Then Jesus put out His hand and touched him,
saying, "I am willing; be cleansed."
Immediately his leprosy was cleansed. And Jesus
said to him, "See that you tell no one; but go
your way, show yourself to the priest, and offer
the gift that Moses commanded, as a testimony
to them" (Matthew 8:3–4).

♦

*Lord, I want to be more and more filled up with
You. Will You continually cleanse me from suspicious
thinking and discomfiture?*

I put forth My hand now, as Jesus stretched
forth His hand and touched the leper, saying,
"Be cleansed." And immediately the leprosy
was gone. Just as speedily, receive an end to all
unproductive thinking and self-consideration.
This is the time! Go your way, showing yourself
only to Me for My commendation and confirmation that it is done. Offer the testimony
when I tell you, to help those grievously tor-
mented by pride and fear. To the degree you believe, it shall be done. (Read Matthew 8:13.)

November 29

◇

Practice Makes Perfect

Therefore gird up the loins of your mind, be sober, and rest your hope fully upon the grace that is to be brought to you at the revelation of Jesus Christ (1 Peter 1:13).

♦

Lord, why is it that I forget so easily Your wondrous words of previous days? How can I feel lack or let my thoughts become fuzzy or tired or busy when You have so often warned me? So often. Just recently You told me to turn—with ceaseless fidelity—to You, and love You more, and always keep the flame of praise burning brightly in my heart. Why is it so hard to draw close to You at the precise moment when I need You most?

Practice moves one toward perfection. Listen! I am holy. And I call on you to be holy. Practice doing the things My Son did when on earth. But beware of Satan's subtle maneuvers. The more you know, the more subtle are his disguises and attempted deceptions. (Read 1 John 2:3.)

◇

Holiness

Then Moses said, "This is the thing which the LORD commanded you to do, and the glory of the LORD will appear to you" (Leviticus 9:6).

♦

When Your worn and weary missionary cried out in New Guinea, asking that You come to him walking on the water, You did. Taking his arm You walked with him on the beach. When he asked if he could sing a song, You answered yes. "O He walks with me and He talks with me," he sang. And, dear Jesus, he said that You wept! That is the splendor of relationship I dearly desire with You, Lord. And I know that You want that depth of faith and love from us, for Your Word says: "Call to Me, and I will answer you, and show you great and mighty things, which you do not know."

My character has not changed, nor My expectations. But the greatest thing you'll ever do is think as I think, will as I will, love as I love, and experience the glory of My presence. (Read Leviticus 11:44–45.)

December

The counsel of the LORD
stands forever, the plans of His
heart to all generations.

Psalm 33:11

December 1

◇

Power and Authority

Then He [Jesus] called His twelve disciples together and gave them power and authority over all demons, and to cure diseases. He sent them to preach the kingdom of God and to heal the sick (Luke 9:1–2).

◆

Thank You, Lord, for Your ultimate patience, for Your power and authority.

I have given you My same power and authority: To cast out unclean spirits, to heal all manner of sickness and disease, to preach, to cleanse, and even to raise the dead. I say again, freely you have received, freely give. I send you forth. Be as wise as a serpent and as harmless and simple as a dove. Beware of men but fear them not, for all that is covered or hidden I shall reveal. And you shall see it and know it. Be not intimidated, for I have overcome the world. Respond only to the prompting of My Holy Spirit. (Read Matthew 10:8; John 16:33.)

Totally Redeemed

To the praise of the glory of His grace, by
which He made us accepted in the Beloved. In
Him we have redemption through His blood,
the forgiveness of sins, according to the riches
of His grace which He made to abound
toward us (Ephesians 1:6–8).

◆

*In sweet adoration, O Lord, I draw near to hear
Your voice, clothed with majesty of fire. I long to be
true to that high and lofty vision of me that You have
in Your great heart.*

For every human being, there is the ideal I
see in him or her: Totally redeemed, free, righteous, and perfect. Often I am disappointed, as
I see even those who are called by My name
crushed by sin. But I am long-suffering, patient,
ceaselessly loving, and forgiving. Strive to be like
Me. (Read Titus 2:11–14.)

December 3

◇

Intimacy with Me

**The blessing of the LORD makes one rich, and
He adds no sorrow with it (Proverbs 10:22).**

◆

*O Lord, thank You for causing Your seed to fall
on fertile ground and take root. Let the harvest be
great, a hundredfold or more. Even as I ask, I care
not for the suffering that may go with it, though I
have heard it causes a specific and great joy known
only by those who suffer with You.*

Fear not, child. The answer lies not so much
in the suffering as in the way one receives and
reacts to it. There is a special joy, a special love
and compassion which grows in those who take
that journey with Me, but it is the close intimacy with Me to which one is driven and not
the suffering itself. Do not wait to draw near, to
praise Me, to believe and act on My Words, to
rest in Me, to listen, to pray, to intercede, to
weep with the weeping, and rejoice with the rejoicing. Do not put off until tomorrow what
you can do today. (Read Hebrews 3:7–8.)

Freely Give

The preparations of the heart belong to man,
but the answer of the tongue is from the LORD.
Commit your works to the LORD, and your
thoughts will be established (Proverbs 16:1, 3).

◆

*Lord, as I have lunch with this person today, fill
me with love and great wisdom. Love, for I am indifferent toward her. Wisdom, to refute the hellish idols
and unsound principles in which she believes.*

Dear one, you have received much, and as
you receive from Me, you must supply the
needs of those I bring to you. Give of your
knowledge, understanding, and patience—not
limiting, not questioning. See only the need.
Go forth, seeing with spiritual eyes. See her suffering. Read behind her eyes and between her
words, not what is evident but the vacancy only
I can fill. See! and be moved by compassion. As
you give love, you most closely resemble Me,
the great giver. Be in no way uncomfortable at
what you face, for I know the answer to all
things. Trust Me in you. (Read Luke 12:12.)

December 5

◇

Calm Assurance

**But those things which proceed out of the
mouth come from the heart, and they
defile a man (Matthew 15:18).**

◆

Lord, help my conversation to be pure.

Those things which proceed out of the
mouth come forth from the heart. Keep your
heart calm, your mind relaxed, for it is life and
health to the body. The work of righteous
hearts shall be peace. The effect of righteous
thinking is quietness and assurance forever. Be
still, and know that I am God. Only when your
heart and mind realize this calm can true and
great work be accomplished. Peace comes from
living with Me. Hearts fail for fear. Let not your
heart be troubled. Let it not be afraid. Gain the
calm I speak of, and keep it at all cost   (Read
Isaiah 32:17.)

Selfishness

He [Jesus] answered and said to them, "When
it is evening you say, 'It will be fair weather, for
the sky is red'; and in the morning, 'It will be
foul weather today, for the sky is red and
threatening.' Hypocrites! You know how
to discern the face of the sky, but you
cannot discern the signs of the
times" (Matthew 16:2–3).

◆

*Lord, help me to discern the times just as clearly
as I discern a storm brewing. Or see the portents even
before the signs appear; even so, I will not depend on
signs, but on You, the Son of the living God.*

Self smothers discernment. Satan endeavors
with all his might to frustrate you in dying to
self, for it is his only entrance to a human mind
or spirit or body. Know his character. Know his
limitations. I am the creative, unlimited, almighty One. By following My lead, you will be
made alert to the first click in the enemy's trap.
(Read 2 Thessalonians 2:9–10.)

December 7

◇

Attack Unbelief

If you have faith as a mustard seed, you will say to this mountain, "Move from here to there," and it will move; and nothing will be impossible for you (Matthew 17:20).

◆

Lord Jesus, strengthen my faith that I may be able to say to the mountain, "Move from here to there," and it will be removed. Only from You does that kind of faith come, Lord. Show me when and how to pray and fast.

Without faith it is impossible to please Me. Fear is a stumbling block to faith, so rout out all fear. Allow perfect love to overtake you, then attack unbelief, that great hinderer, by prayer and fasting. (Read Mark 10:52.)

December 8

◇

Seek Me

Then Peter came to Him and said, "Lord, how often shall my brother sin against me, and I forgive him? Up to seven times?" Jesus said to him, "I do not say to you, up to seven times, but up to seventy times seven" (Matthew 18:21–22).

◆

Lord, help me to heed Your word to me. Help me to be aware of You every moment.

Again I say to you, you shall know Me when you seek Me with all your heart. And likewise, forgive *anyone anything,* for it is My will. It is the only way to grow in My Kingdom. Anyone means yourself, as well. Respect your life and temple, for it houses My Holy Spirit. (Read Matthew 7:7–8.)

December 9

◇

Follow Christ

**Be still, and know that I am God; I will
be exalted among the nations, I will be
exalted in the earth! (Psalm 46:10).**

◆

*Lord, thank You for Your goodness and mercy and
grace. Thank You for our daughter's marriage,
which was officially announced tonight as we decor-
ated the Christmas tree. You are so good, Father.*

Your hopes and your prayers have been re-
warded. And opportunities for works in My
name will increase because of this union. As
they recognize My Godhead, they shall teach
the truths of My Kingdom to others, for in
those truths they shall be living and working.
They shall by their lives, sufferings, words, and
love prove to the questing ones that the search
will end in Me. Jesus left the saving of souls to
commune with Me, the Father. Tell them to go
and do likewise. Instruct them to follow Christ
into the quiet places of prayer. To rest. To be still
and know that I am God. Then rise and go in
My name. . . . (Read 1 John 2:15–17.)

Love

Jesus said to him, "'You shall love the LORD your God with all your heart, with all your soul, and with all your mind.' This is the first and great commandment. And the second is like it: 'You shall love your neighbor as yourself'" (Matthew 22:37–39).

♦

Precious Savior, I believe everything You say. Strengthen our children's faith, cause the wind of Your Spirit to blow away all doubts, and give them a belief in You and Your promises that cannot be shaken.

Tell them to know the Scriptures, and know My power. My greatest commandment is "Love the Lord your God with all your heart, and with all your soul, and with all your mind." And the second greatest is "Love your neighbor as yourself." It is right to love and respect one's self. The proof that one does is how full that one is of Me. Tell them when they need more faith, more love, more strength, more patience, more fulfillment, to praise Me more—and it shall surely come. (Read Philippians 4:8–9.)

December 11

◇

All Health

**And whoever exalts himself will be humbled,
and he who humbles himself will be
exalted (Matthew 23:12).**

◆

*Lord Jesus, You are our example. Show us how to
serve as You did when on earth. Some say that one
learns through suffering and sickness, which is no
doubt true. And yet, the Scriptures record no case of
Your being diseased or ill.*

The greatest among you shall be the servant.
Give to the poor, and make no pretense at
prayer. Tithe, judge wisely and with compassion, be merciful in all things, and be great in
faith. Strain not over small things. Cleanse first
that which is within, that the outside may be
clean also. Let no hypocrisy overtake you, but
be righteous! Let your actions mean what they
appear to mean, neither hidden nor manipula-
tive, nor excessive in any way. Be not one who
seeks to impress but one who is honest to God
and man, honorable and upright. This is the
way of health. (Read 1 Peter 2:11–12.)

Know My Word

"Therefore when you see the 'abomination of desolation,' spoken of by Daniel the prophet, standing in the holy place" (whoever reads, let him understand), . . . "And unless those days were shortened, no flesh would be saved; but for the elect's sake those days will be shortened" (Matthew 24:15, 22).

◆

Lord, You have shown us in Your Word the signs of the end times. Even facing affliction, hatred, or death, cause us not to betray one another, to return hate, to be deceived by false prophets, or to allow our love—for You, ourselves, and others—to grow cold. Show us how to endure to the end.

Watch! For only the redeemed shall understand when the Son of Man comes and sends His angels to gather the elect. As the lightning, so shall the coming of Christ be. Heaven and earth shall pass away but My Word will not. My Word either validates or invalidates whatever you hear and see. Know My Word! (Read 1 Corinthians 10:11; Daniel 9:27; 12:1.)

December 13

◇

Talents

His lord said to him, "Well done, good and faithful servant; you were faithful over a few things, I will make you ruler over many things. Enter into the joy of your lord. . . . For to everyone who has, more will be given, and he will have abundance; but from him who does not have, even what he has will be taken away" (Matthew 25:21, 29).

◆

Lord, You have given me many talents, for which I heartily thank You. I want to multiply them, Father, so that when You come You will say to me, "Well done, good and faithful servant."

Know My heart. Trust Me completely, doubting not. Doubt leads to fear, and those who fear are not capable of multiplying the talents I have given. No one has been overlooked. Fear of failure and fear of success are born of pride. Listen! Unto every one who has shall be given abundance; but the unprofitable servant who does not use his talent shall lose it. (Read James 1:5–8.)

December 14

◇

Peace

**He will not allow your foot to be moved; He
who keeps you will not slumber. Behold, He
who keeps Israel shall neither slumber
nor sleep (Psalm 121:3–4).**

◆

*Lord, help our children to walk with constant
awareness of Your presence. As the tempests rage, or
the busyness overtakes, let them remain unmoved.*

It is My wish for them. And I have given
them every tool. I want them to be as a cool
garden with fragrant flowers, humming bees,
butterflies and shade trees and ferns, playing
fountains and sunspotted fresh air, set in the
midst of a roaring, polluted city. Tell them to
see their lives more and more as a sanctuary.
Calm and unmoved. Unrushed. Assured.
Peaceful. Trusting. Expressing beauty and joy. A
refuge for My poor, weary, empty, anguished
world. Tell them: I am peace. Let My love reign.
Rest in Me. Be all I have made you to be. Fear
not. I love you. (Read Psalm 34:14; Ephesians
2:14.)

December 15

◇

Start with Praise

Because Your lovingkindness is better than life,
my lips shall praise You. Thus I will bless You
while I live; I will lift up my hands in Your
name. My soul shall be satisfied as with marrow
and fatness, and my mouth shall praise You
with joyful lips. When I remember You on my
bed, I meditate on You in the night watches.
Because You have been my help, therefore in
the shadow of Your wings I will rejoice
(Psalm 63:3–7).

◆

*Guide me, Lord, not according to my plan but
Yours. I do not want to be found sleeping when You
come. When You want me, I want to be ready.*

The spirit is willing but the flesh is weak.
Start with praise! for it opens your awareness to
Me. Discipline yourself to prayer. Even when
you do not feel the thrill or joy you think should
accompany worship, do it anyway, and the sunshine of My Spirit will penetrate the cloud
cover. Joy and calm will surely come. And you
will be ready! (Read Romans 15:13.)

December 16

◇

Without Doubt

And Jesus came and spoke to them, saying, "All authority has been given to Me in heaven and on earth" (Matthew 28:18).

◆

O risen Lord, answer our prayer for more faith. Cause our doubts to be buried and Your faith to be resurrected in our hearts and minds.

You are about to see Me in a new light . . . the same, yet different. You shall see Me and worship Me, without doubt . . . as never before. I will come and I will speak to you. All power is given unto Me in heaven and on earth, and My power is your power. Even so, I am about to show you a new thing. Expect it, for your expectations will not be disappointed. I am with you always, but your understanding will be opened to My presence in a new way. (Read Psalm 116:1–2.)

December 17

◇

Order

**Now in the morning, having risen a long while
before daylight, He went out and departed
to a solitary place; and there He prayed
(Mark 1:35).**

◆

Lord, show me Your order for the day.

The right order: Rising early in the morning,
departing into a solitary place with Me before
the day begins, praising Me, praying, loving Me,
breathing the breath of My Holy Spirit, giving
Me the moments . . . there are no substitutes . . . therein is the power, the strength, and
the motivation. (Read Psalm 63:1–3.)

Commitment

Then He appointed twelve, that they might be with Him and that He might send them out to preach, and to have power to heal sicknesses and to cast out demons (Mark 3:14–15).

♦

Dear Lord, You ordained twelve that they should be with You, go forth to preach, have the power to heal sicknesses, cast out devils. We say today: We will go wherever You send us.

You shall see wonders, ask wonders, bear wonders away with you, for in your home I feel welcome. I shall send My servants and leaders, as well as those who only need to rest, or need the ear of a friend . . . to be loved and fed spiritual food. But be released. I will do the planning, and I will make the final outcome. All you have to do is commit your whole self to Me so that My plan will succeed. (Read Proverbs 16:3.)

◇

Armed for Conflict

Finally, my brethren, be strong in the Lord and
in the power of His might. Put on the whole
armor of God, that you may be able to
stand against the wiles of the devil
(Ephesians 6:10–11).

◆

*Father, give us that perfect way of overcoming
weariness, sickness, disease, unrest, and busyness at
this wondrous Christmas season. Make us hopeful in
facing all the chaos of the world. Show us how to
maintain our peace and balance in these times, how
to rule our own spirits, how to disallow all fear. Prepare us now for the days ahead with You.*

First put on the garment of praise to cushion
My armor. The helmet of salvation to protect
the mind and emotions, the breastplate of righteousness for your attitudes and motives.
Girded about with truth, walk in shoes of peace.
Carry the shield of faith. Finally, take My Word:
believe it, hide it in your heart, cling to it. It
is mighty for the pulling down of strongholds.
(Read Ephesians 6:13.)

◇

Be Whole

Wherever He entered, into villages, cities, or the country, they laid the sick in the marketplaces, and begged Him that they might just touch the hem of His garment. And as many as touched Him were made well (Mark 6:56).

◆

Great things You have done for me, O Lord, and Your compassion is new every morning.

Yes, virtue has gone out of Me to you, beloved. Be whole. Receive wholesome faith. Let every act of Mine stir, renew, and add to your trust. Let nothing tear down, erode, or in any way destroy the cords of love that bind Me to you. Wholeness is gained by coming apart into a desert place with Me and resting a while, privately gleaning from your Shepherd, your Rabbi, your Teacher. Be always of good cheer, never troubled. As many as touch Me are made whole. Continue to touch Me; and My virtue will continue to flow to you. (Read Matthew 8:13.)

December 21

◇

Seek My Truth

Then Jesus said to those Jews who believed
Him, "If you abide in My word, you are My
disciples indeed. And you shall know the truth,
and the truth shall make you free"
(John 8:31–32).

◆

*Lord, make us wise to what we hear, finely tuned
to the truth. As radar detects any foreign or odd vessels
in its range, let our antennae be so sensitive that they
instantly detect falsity and perceive clearly Your truth.*

I rejoice at those who seek My truth. And
their sleep will be sweet who obey it. Also, they
are wise, and from their minds come careful,
persuasive speech. And self-control, which is
greater than the control of a network, news-
paper, or city. Only when you have control of
yourself can you hand over the controls to Me.
(Read Psalm 51:6; Proverbs 16:32.)

Fear of the Lord

**The fear of the LORD is the beginning of
knowledge, but fools despise wisdom
and instruction (Proverbs 1:7).**

◆

*Because man now has the capability to destroy all
of mankind, he no longer seems to fear Your wrath,
Lord. Let reverence for You have its proper place in
us, for You have told us that "fear of the Lord is the
beginning of knowledge."*

And so it is. It shall be health to your body,
strength and lubricant to your bones, and life to
the mind and emotions. You will also walk
safely, lie down without being afraid, and experience a sleep that is serene and restorative. My
Word in your heart is vitalizing and procreative
to all your flesh . . . out of your heart flow the
springs of life. Keep your mouth and lips from
speaking any perversity, for you are snared by
the words of your mouth. (Read Proverbs
3:7–8; Matthew 12:37.)

December 23

◇

Spend Your Life

Jesus said to him, "If you can believe, all things
are possible to him who believes." So He said to
them, "This kind can come out by nothing but
prayer and fasting" (Mark 9:23, 29).

♦

*Lord Jesus, when You walked the earth You
healed the sick and restored sight to the blind. You
delivered from hellish bondage, cast out deaf and
dumb spirits, and made men, women, and children
whole wherever Your feet stepped. Why are there so
few miracles today through Your servants, Lord?*

Lack of discipline in fasting, prayer, and giving of self; add to that unbelief and My servants'
lack of compassion. I did not have to stir up
compassion when the need arose. It is part of
My Being. My very character. My servants are
not ready to give up their lives for another.
Know that My power will accomplish that for
which you pray. Only those willing to give all
will accomplish lovingly and compassionately
the big things in prayer. The big and little are all
the same to Me. (Read Matthew 17:20–21.)

◇

Faith

Then Jesus said to him, "Go your way; your faith has made you well." And immediately he received his sight and followed Jesus on the road (Mark 10:52).

◆

You say the big and the little are all the same to You, Lord, so I ask for Your loving, healing mercies to be extended to the handicapped lady in our church; in the name of our Lord and Savior, Jesus Christ of Nazareth, whose birthday we celebrate tomorrow. Let faith arise in her heart, in the hearts of our companions, and in our hearts.

When you pray, enter as a little child, humble in worship of the Bethlehem Babe! Enter as among the earth's lowliest. Then let repentance flow. Remember when you prayed for the bird to have life restored? It was only after you confessed that you were more concerned with your faith being rebuilt than with the bird being healed, that it happened. Think on that! Then step out beside Me . . . your faith will make others whole. (Read Mark 11:24–25.)

December 25

◇

Happy Birthday, Jesus

Jesus answered and said to him, "If anyone loves Me, he will keep My word; and My Father will love him, and We will come to him and make Our home with him. He who does not love Me does not keep My words; and the word which you hear is not Mine but the Father's who sent Me" (John 14:23–24).

◆

Happy birthday, dear Jesus. Thank You for leaving Your heavenly place to come to this cold and desolate planet that we might have life eternal. Oh, how great Thou art! Hosanna, blessed and humble King! Let me sit adoringly, Lord, and just love You, not asking but giving.

If you love Me, you will keep My commandments. And take Me at My Word. You have it on My authority . . . the highest authority. (Read Matthew 28:18.)

Joy in My Presence

And you shall love the LORD your God with all your heart, with all your soul, with all your mind, and with all your strength (Mark 12:30).

◆

My Lord and my God, how wonderful You are. Thank You for the blessed day of Christmas with our children, and especially for my husband, wise and healthy and at peace. Thank You for the capacity You have given him to enjoy, that holidays are no longer anathema to him. Only You know how grateful I am. Thank You for the absence of pain and suffering this Christmas in all our family. But most of all, Lord, thank You for Yourself, and all You know Yourself to be . . . and for our awareness of You.

Live in the joy of My constant presence, beloved. Yield every moment to Me. Live in the present! Give Me all your thoughts and your service will be glorious—your mind clear, your attitude calm and patient, at ease with others and yourself, transparent before Me, single of eye and intent. (Read Proverbs 16:3.)

December 27

◇

Watch and Pray

Watch therefore, for you do not know when the master of the house is coming—in the evening, at midnight, at the crowing of the rooster, or in the morning—lest, coming suddenly, he find you sleeping. And what I say to you, I say to all: Watch! (Mark 13:35–37).

◆

Lord, I want to remember Your instruction and Your Word exactly, with a right spirit to follow and obey. What must I do to be constant?

Take heed to what I have told you. Watch and pray! I say unto you, Watch! Stay ready for Me, as if I were on your doorstep. Sing songs and psalms daily. Say, as I said to Our Father, "All things are possible through You . . . not what I want but what You want." To Peter, John, and James, I said, "Could you not watch one hour? Watch and pray, lest you enter into temptation." The spirit is truly ready, but the flesh is weak. Beloved, the hour is come for perseverance as never before. Rise up, leaving self behind, and let us go! (Read Mark 14:37–38.)

Knowing Is Better

For I am the LORD, I do not change; therefore you are not consumed, O sons of Jacob (Malachi 3:6).

◆

Lord, how injured You must have been when Judas added to the betrayal by kissing You and calling You Master. Perhaps Peter's denial hurt You even more. Or was it my sin, when I turned my back on You, my own hardness of heart? O Jesus . . . thank You for Your forgiving presence.

Beloved, feelings are good, but do not put your trust in them, for they can be false. Feelings are of the flesh, the mind, and the emotions, and make one conscious of self, whereas God-consciousness is of My Spirit and of your spirit. Your feeling that I am or am not with you can be deceiving, for it may be the result of a passing mood or change of circumstance. I am not influenced by situations that change . . . I am always the same. You can trust My Word. Believe Me. Feeling is all right but *knowing* is better. (Read Hebrews 13:8.)

December 29

◇

Encouragement

**For with God nothing will be impossible
(Luke 1:37).**

◆

*Give me confidence, O Lord, to finish the tasks
You have labeled as mine in this life. I want Your
priorities to be my priorities. Let not the urgent things
take precedent over the most important.*

I was with you, beloved, even in the days
when you chose to be unaware of Me. Now that
you walk in worshipful service, would I forsake
you? Fear not. Ponder My Word deeply: Rejoice
in it, sing it, think it in silence, allow My zeal to
perform it. Quietly, patiently welcome the Holy
Ghost, and let rest on the ledge of your mind
always the thought: With God nothing is impossible.

According to Thy will, Lord, I believe.

(Read Psalm 119:15–16.)

Obedience

**But Mary kept all these things and pondered
them in her heart (Luke 2:19).**

◆

*Dear Jesus, I want to be more like You, and like
Your Father, and like Your mother, by the power of
the Holy Ghost.*

My mother kept all things concerning Me
and pondered them in her heart. She went for
the purification, without taking any credit for
her part in the miracle birth of the Messiah. Yes,
be more like her, while serving My Father with
fastings and prayers night and day, as Anna did.
And yes, be like Me, the child who grew, strong
in spirit, filled with wisdom and the grace of
God. I had understanding and answers, for I
was about My Father's business, increasing always in wisdom. Listen to the Father! He is calling you to a deeper level of constancy and
understanding than ever before. What better
place in all the world to learn these principles
than the land of My birth, the city called Holy?
Blessed Jerusalem! (Read Luke 2:40, 52.)

December 31

◇

Seek Him—Now Is the Time

And Jesus answered and said to him, . . . "It is written, 'You shall worship the LORD your God, and Him only you shall serve'" (Luke 4:8).

◆

Holy One of Israel, life-transforming, deeper revelation from You I lay on the altar of this year's end. While I do pray for it, I give up any struggle for it. Save me, O creative One, and purify me from taking notice of any part I have in Your miracles.

It is written, you shall worship the Lord your God, and Him only shall you serve. As you worship and serve Him, all that He has for you shall be given. And when you speak My name, "Jesus," I will lift your spirit to the top of the Judean hills, where I overcame the greatest temptations Satan could offer. Open your spirit to the Holy Spirit, who will anoint you for all that you are meant to do . . . as He anointed Me. This is the time. Now is the hour! (Read Acts 4:31; 10:38.)